INTERNATIONAL LIQUIDITY

International Liquidity

A STUDY IN THE ECONOMIC
FUNCTIONS OF GOLD

IAN SHANNON

HENRY REGNERY COMPANY
CHICAGO

*Originally published in 1964
by F. W. Cheshire Pty. Ltd., Australia
Regnery edition copyright 1966,
Henry Regnery Company*

Printed in the United States of America

Library of Congress Catalog Card No. 66-16512

PREFACE

Over the last year it has become increasingly apparent that the function of international reserves is normally considered to be only a monetary one. Banking and treasury officials are nowadays concerned about international monetary arrangements, not because they fear the existing system may be unable to cope with both the current and future economic needs, but simply because the American dollar is in difficulties. The aim of the present study is to redress some of the balance by painting the functions of international liquidity within a fairly wide canvas of economic characteristics. Since the monetary systems should be the servant and not the master of man's economic destiny, no other approach would seem to give a basis for making intelligent estimates about future international liquidity requirements.

My earlier book, *The Economic Functions of Gold*, was first published in 1962 and much water has flowed under the international liquidity bridge since then. New important studies have also added to the statistical material available and gaps in our information are no longer so striking. For this reason further reprints of the earlier book seemed less appropriate than a new look at the topic taking account of more recent thinking of others as well as myself. Although the first four chapters of the present study are partly based on *The Economic Functions of Gold*, the subsequent sections are new and attempt to bring the crucial economic challenges facing the free world into focus with the desirable monetary objectives.

Mrs. Jocelyn Howlett has again given me much help in the preparation of the present study. My thanks are due to her, and to Dr. J. O. N. Perkins of the University of Melbourne for casting his penetrating eye upon the earlier drafts. The expression of opinion nevertheless remains my responsibility.

IAN SHANNON

CONTENTS

TABLES

CHAPTER I

GOLD: THE BASIC INTERNATIONAL MONEY

Gold is international money. Because it is acceptable over national boundaries a country may keep gold as a reserve to meet net international debts. Such forms of national money as dollars and sterling are also used as international money but they are nevertheless essentially the domestic currency of the United States and the United Kingdom. Historically gold has also been both national and international money, but during the last hundred years particularly it has gradually been withdrawn from domestic circulation in all countries. For this reason gold as international money nowadays bears a close resemblance to the various suggested forms of new international paper obligations such as J. M. Keynes's *bancor*. The essential idea is that the use of such money will also be limited to international banking transactions.

New supplies of gold are limited by the facts of geology and the profitability of mining the metal at a selling price of $35 an ounce. The supply of gold is therefore determined by geology and engineering rather than by monetary requirements. Over the last century cancelling the net debts of international trading has proved well beyond the capacity of the gold mining industry, for great political upheavals and an extraordinary technical revolution have brought a dramatic increase in world business and in the demand for international liquidity.

As the supply of an international paper obligation could be tailored more exactly to fit international monetary needs, such a system may appear to be more sensible than depending upon the output of gold, limited as it is by nature. But humanity generally

1

and central bankers in particular seem to regard the whims of nature as being more becoming than the whims of man, and for this and other reasons the development of a purely international paper currency is unlikely soon to appear as accepted reality. The interim is the difficult period, for in a world of imperfect international understanding and co-operation, the evolution towards a more sophisticated international monetary system is subject to national interests and suspicions. It is not difficult to find many problems attendant upon using national currencies such as the dollar as international money, and the world is still essentially dependent upon gold as the ultimate monetary store of value and medium of exchange.

Thus the monetary tradition of a thousand odd years is still maintained. Yet the concept of the gold standard tradition is a modern development. Its origins in Western Europe date back to the England of the Elizabethans. From this period much of the piecemeal evolution towards the gold standard of the later nineteenth century occurred. It was complicated by the relative exchange values between gold and silver in the bimetallic system then prevalent. Different countries adopted varying exchange values between gold and silver, and this created arbitrage problems somewhat on the lines of contemporary difficulties occurring in the exchange markets. Sir Isaac Newton in an attempt to overcome this problem in 1715 set the legal exchange ratio between gold and silver at 1 to 15 in one of his lesser known and less valid "laws". Such a ratio between the two metals meant that for large transactions over greater distances silver had distinct disadvantages.[1]

Largely for this reason, and with a steady expansion in trade and banking, the use of silver was confined more and more to smaller and localized transactions. In 1871 Bismarck adopted a new currency for Germany, the gold mark to replace the silver thaler. In the process Germany started buying gold and selling silver in huge amounts, and therefore changed the customary price relationship between the two metals. The reform was also

[1] For instance, a thousand gold guineas weighed 18½lb. (avoirdupois) while the same value in silver weighed nearly 2¾cwt. (R. G. Hawtrey, *The Gold Standard in Theory and Practice*, London, Longmans Green and Co., fifth edition, 1947, p. 79.)

a mortal blow to silver's monetary role, for one of the essential characteristics of any reserve, whether represented in metal or paper claims, is that it should not depreciate in relation to alternative reserve mediums. The price change meant that the currencies of silver-using countries began to depreciate in terms of gold as the ratio between the two metals moved further and further away from Sir Isaac Newton's determination. By 1903 the ratio between gold and silver was 1 to 43.[2]

The United States was on a bimetallic gold and silver standard from the founding of the Republic, excluding only the period of the inconvertible paper "greenbacks" in circulation during and after the Civil War.[3] Since 1873 the United States dollar has been defined in terms of gold and silver. Although the United States is nowadays replacing its silver certificates with a note issue from the Federal Reserve—and thus reducing the required cover in scarce silver—the process nevertheless increases the domestic gold commitment, for Federal Reserve notes need a 25 per cent gold backing.[4] Other countries avoid bimetallic difficulties of this nature by using silver only in token coinage and most European countries adopted the international gold standard over the thirty years between 1870 and 1900. Japan was also a member of this group but other Eastern countries delayed their change to a gold base until after the first world war.

The development towards the predominance of gold and the stability in exchange transactions during the forty years before 1914 was the result of centuries of monetary experimentation. Even its success over this short period was at least partly the result of two historical accidents. Britain was at the nucleus of the system, and with a focal point based on the political and economic strength of London, the international monetary system had a concentration which has since been dispersed. Secondly, the gold standard system and the financing of world trade was greatly facilitated by the discovery of gold in the new world. The world's stock of monetary gold is estimated to have trebled

[2] In 1964, New York buying prices for gold and silver yielded a ratio of 1 to 27.

[3] Oscar L. Altman, "The Role of Gold in International Liquidity", *The Mines Magazine* (U.S.), October 1960, p. 39.

[4] See International Monetary Fund, *Annual Report, 1963*, Washington, D.C., pp. 183-4.

3

between 1867 and 1913.[5] Even though the next half-century witnessed a greater lift in gold production, with monetary reserves of gold rising just on six times in volume, other changes were more remarkable.

GOLD AS A MONETARY STANDARD

Although it is possible to distinguish a wide range of monetary standards, there are essentially three possible gold standards.[6] The "ideal" of the various gold systems is one which can be allowed to regulate the economic system without official intervention. This is generally assumed to be possible under the PURE GOLD STANDARD (frequently called the gold specie standard) where the central authority buys or sells gold in unlimited quantities at legally fixed prices. Gold coins circulate freely, banknotes are redeemable in gold, and there are no restrictions on holding gold or on its movement in both domestic and foreign trade. If the system is to maintain full convertibility, the pure gold standard has a set of rules which cannot be substantially violated. A nation on the standard, for example, should refrain from interference in the flows of foreign trade through implementing such devices as import quotas, bounties, and high tariffs.

The GOLD BULLION STANDARD, as originally postulated by David Ricardo, has all the "rules" of the gold specie standard but in this case bank-notes are not redeemable in gold, and gold coins are not circulated. Ricardo described the idea of the gold bullion standard in his *Proposals for an Economical and Secure Currency* of 1816 with the aim of ensuring a concentration of all available gold into reserves. Nevertheless, to allow the system to remain as close as possible to the ideal of the pure gold standard, under the gold bullion standard there is an obligation for the central bank to buy and sell gold bars without restriction

[5] J. M. Keynes, *Treatise on Money*, London, Macmillan and Co., 1930, Vol. II, p. 296.

[6] Pierre R. Hines, writing for *Gold and Money Session* of the 1960 AIME Pacific Northwest Metals and Minerals Conference, Portland, Oregon, pp. 1-2, distinguishes no less than six monetary standards. These are the gold standard, gold coin and gold bullion standard, bimetallic standard, managed paper standard, silver standard and the gold exchange standard.

at fixed prices. In 1918 the Cunliffe Committee thought highly of the idea and recommended this scheme for Britain. When this country returned to gold in 1925 the Bank of England was obliged to sell gold to all comers provided they could afford the cash payment for the 400 fine ounce minimum order. With the system re-established in the inter-war years, the free import and export of gold was allowed and, although the concept of full convertibility remained, the demand for gold for internal circulation was adequately prevented.[7]

Under the third (and present-day) system of the GOLD EXCHANGE STANDARD there is no obligation for central banks to sell gold bars, nor need the bank-notes in circulation be redeemable. With the aim of moving as much gold as possible into official hoards for international usage, the national currency issue entirely replaces the use of gold for domestic transactions. The size of official monetary reserves may be further extended under the gold exchange standard through the use of certain national obligations such as dollars and sterling as international reserves alongside gold. But as noted in Chapter VII, the use of dollars and sterling as international reserves—frequently called the key currency component of reserves—can also create problems hindering the smooth functioning of the international monetary system.

The holding of key currencies in addition to gold has its origin in Russia before the turn of the last century although, as will be described in Chapter II, its use as accepted practice stems from the Genoa Conference of 1922. In fact, at the beginning of the first world war only 10 per cent of all international reserves were held in foreign exchange, while before the crash of the inter-war gold exchange standard some 42 per cent of total reserves were composed of exchange in the high tide year of 1928.[8] In June 1965 the proportion of reserves in the form of exchange was 27 per cent.

Since the operation of the international monetary system over the period since 1913 has been rather haphazard, if not distinctly unsatisfactory, a great many economic philosophers and a few economic theorists plead for a return to the pure gold standard. Instead of solving the world's international monetary problems,

[7] R. G. Hawtrey, *op. cit.*, pp. 58-9.
[8] See Table 2, p. 26.

tinkering about with the monetary machinery over the last fifty years seems to have increased the world's economic difficulties. From the distance of a half-century, pre-1914 now seems a placid, civilized era compared with the turbulence of contemporary affairs.

Whether true or not, this view of the past ignores the immense social and economic changes since 1913 and the quite different contemporary environment. For one thing the gold standard of the later nineteenth century was strongly based on free trade. In the system pivoted on London, British loans to primary exporting countries enabled them to increase their purchases while their debt service payments so equalized the transaction that Britain did not lose much gold through the loan transfer.[9] In fact, compared with the volume of international transactions little gold was needed during this period. Then secondly, the primary exporting countries had few payments problems—at least in theory—for the growing British market meant that an increase in their export sales could cover debt service charges plus an increase in manufacturing imports from Britain. In the free trade environment, both trade and capital flows contributed to balance of payments stability. The contemporary world by contrast is extraordinarily different: not only does agricultural protectionism in Western Europe and North America and the drive to industrialization in the so-called periphery countries increase the difficulties of maintaining balance in world payments, but foreign military expenditure and some economic aid entails a considerable international movement of funds not necessarily dovetailing into a pattern of payments arising from commerce.

But, perhaps most important, economic welfare must be subordinated to the rules of the system if the pure gold standard system is to work. There is nothing assured, for example, about the gold standard system giving price stability. Indeed if a country is receiving gold it should be willing to inflate prices regardless of dislocation. Similarly, when a gold drain occurs, the necessary action is deflation through reduced prices, incomes and employment. Even with these disadvantages the gold standard in any case did not necessarily restore a country's external position. For

[9] A. G. Ford, *The Gold Standard 1880-1914; Britain and Argentina*, Oxford University Press, 1962, p. 28.

one thing the theory of the way the system worked implies a direct link with the quantity theory of money. For another, it assumes that short-term changes in national income cause similar changes in the expenditure on imports.

In any case in the pre-1914 period the corrective influence of gold movements on price levels was not so great as is frequently imagined, for otherwise there would have been great cycles of inflation and deflation. Owing to the complementary nature of world trade and payments, little gold actually moved from country to country. Again, domestic and international prices tended to be cemented together because there was a common element in the price of internationally traded commodities in an essentially free trade world. The price stabilizing ability of the gold standard was never really put to the test. In fact the gold standard grew from a particular set of circumstances which caused it to flower in the late nineteenth century; any attempt to transplant the system to the contemporary world would simply be introducing it to a completely different and unfriendly environment.

Loose talk about a return to the gold standard can conjure up further confusion for there is a variety of gold standards and one such standard in fact operates today—the gold exchange standard. Even over the forty years to 1914 there was certainly no uniformity in the gold standard idea. Wide variations were to be found both in legal requirements and institutional practice; some countries (e.g. Britain, Germany, and the United States) had a full gold standard, others (e.g. France) possessed a "limping" gold standard, under which the monetary authorities had the option of exchanging notes into gold or into full legal-tender silver coins, whilst others (e.g. Russia, Japan, much of the British Empire) adhered to varieties of gold exchange standard, holding much of their international reserves in the form of foreign currency.'[10] During this period it was also common practice for the Bank of England to use the dominance of the London market in altering the bank rate to attract gold and capital flows to Britain from other countries.

Even in more recent times there has been great confusion about the concept of "the gold standard". For instance during

[10] Ford, *op. cit.*, p. 18.

the 1914-18 war it was generally accepted in Britain that the country was on the gold standard because internal convertibility was maintained although the export of gold was prohibited. But in 1925, in a striking turnabout, a return to the gold standard was suddenly proclaimed by making gold externally convertible even though its internal use was effectively controlled.[11]

Although external convertibility between gold and designated national currencies provides the basis for the treasury and banking concepts of a gold standard, domestic convertibility and the circulation of gold coinage has remained the most important aspect of the more general philosophy about "being on the gold standard". The divergence between these approaches has caused much confusion. When looking at the inter-war years, for example, Brown noted that, 'to Americans the most striking feature of the gold bullion standard was that foreigners were allowed to take gold while this right was denied to American citizens, whereas to Europeans its most striking feature was that it secured all the benefits of the "full" gold standard and at the same time economized gold'.[12]

The present-day monetary use of gold is further complicated by a variety of domestic currency reserve systems, no matter what type of standard is suggested. As far as currency laws in individual countries are concerned, the reserves backing the note issue may range all the way from an interchange of alternative bits of paper, either foreign or domestic, through to 100 per cent gold backing. In theory, if not in practice, the higher the percentage of gold cover required to fulfil the historical role of maintaining confidence in paper money, the lower the proportion available for use as international reserves. The precise level of legal currency reserve ratios in different countries, as well as its composition, is largely based on convention, habit and a reluctance to depart from the accepted practice. With the breakdown of the gold standard during the first world war, the reserve ratio system became fairly common practice. Gold cover requirements are still enforced in France, Belgium, Switzerland, the Netherlands and the United States.

[11] W. A. Brown, Jr., *The International Gold Standard Re-interpreted 1914-34*, New York, National Bureau of Economic Research, 1940, p. 382.
[12] *ibid.*

Viewed in relation to the monetary functions of gold—and particularly in relation to its scarcity—the case of the United States is by far the most important. At the beginning of 1964 some $12 billion in gold was required to meet the 25 per cent legal cover requirements for the United States note issue, this sum being equal to 77 per cent of the United States total gold reserves at that time and just over 30 per cent of total free world gold reserves.[13]

In the United Kingdom, on the other hand, sterling bank-notes are normally issued against the backing of marketable government securities. This amounts to the exchange of arbitrarily valued pieces of paper. In any case the Radcliffe Committee suggested, 'the authorities . . . do not regard the supply of bank-notes as being the only, nor nowadays the only important, supply of money, and the Government's function in issuing notes is simply the passive one of ensuring that sufficient notes are available for the practical convenience of the public'.[14] But misgivings about the effects of the volume of currency money on prices still persist in most countries even though it is the total supply of money (of which currency is only a small proportion) that influences demand and prices. Hence the braking power of any provision for part or all of the currency to be backed by gold is relatively ineffective, and particularly in countries like the United States where currency constitutes only one-fifth of the total money supply.

[13] Amending legislation was introduced into the United States House of Representatives in May 1961 in an attempt to release gold held as cover against the domestic note issue for the more urgent and important cover of dollar exchange assets held by other countries. Despite Treasury endorsement these Bills met with great opposition and were dropped. What international reserves lose through domestic currency cover requirements may not be so important in practice as in principle. The late President Kennedy's inaugural statements implied that the United States domestic reserves would be used in an emergency. The political implications of a change in gold legislation make it difficult for any Administration to alter the price at a time of its own choosing. The most likely time for a change is at the beginning of a new term of office. The events of 1960 were connected with a speculative interest in the actions of a new President.

[14] United Kingdom, *Report of the Committee on the Working of the Monetary System*, 1959, Cmd. 827, para. 348, p. 118.

B

THE LEAKAGE OF MONETARY GOLD

Gold remains in short supply because the growth in the mining output of the metal has been insufficient to service the irregularities in world payments which have themselves resulted from rapid economic and political changes. At the same time a large proportion of newly mined gold is used for non-monetary purposes, the net result being a triangle of interests between official hoarders, hoarders on private account, and those wishing to employ the metal for industrial and artistic pursuits.

Legal restrictions on the private ownership of gold have found their origins in the shortage of the metal and the co-aligned need to mobilize as much as possible into central reserves. Even in those countries where the ownership of gold is permitted, there are restrictions associated with exporting the metal and particularly to certain countries. The world is therefore a long way from one aspect of the gold specie standard. Certainly, and as shown in Table 1 below, few Western countries permit the free ownership and movement of gold. This has greatest relevance in the case of the United States and the United Kingdom for these are the two key currency countries with the greatest call on their official reserves.

TABLE 1

Gold Regulations in Various Countries

	Ownership At home	Allowed Abroad	Free Trading within Country
United Kingdom	No	No	No[1]
United States	No[2]	No	No
France	Yes	No	Yes
Switzerland	Yes	Yes	Yes
West Germany	Yes	Yes	Yes[3]
Belgium	Yes	Yes	Yes

Notes: [1] Trading on London market free for non-residents of sterling area.
[2] Coins minted before 1933 permitted.
[3] 4 per cent tax on all internal gold purchases.

Source: Adapted from *The Economist*, 29 October 1960, p. 475.

Gold: The Basic International Money

The International Monetary Fund, since its inception, has maintained the Bretton Woods doctrine that stocks of gold should be concentrated in the hands of central banks or treasuries, and it has demurred at any leakage to private hoardings.[15] Yet during the post-war years the Fund has been unable to prevent the re-establishment of a series of gold markets. The re-opening of the London market in 1954 marked an end to a series of attempts to move all gold through official hands.

According to Busschau, only seven out of every ten ounces of gold mined over the 125 years between 1835 and 1959 have moved into official reserves.[16] At least 12 per cent moved into private hoards, while industry and the arts absorbed the remainder of approximately 20 per cent. In more recent years the statistics suggest that official monetary stocks are receiving a lesser share of new supplies (i.e. newly mined gold plus Russian gold sales to the West). Robert Triffin has estimated that over the five years from 1952 to 1957, official reserves gained just over 52 per cent of total supplies while 19 per cent went to industry and the arts, with the balance of 29 per cent going to private hoards.[17] Although it is most difficult to reconcile the various estimates showing the quantity of new gold moving into private hoards, without a doubt the proportion hoarded fluctuates violently—but generally seems to have been rising. The International Monetary Fund figures for 1960 indicate that 24 per cent of new supplies went to official reserves. In 1961 official monetary stocks received 42 per cent, while in 1962 private hoarding plus consumption for industry and the arts took no less than four-fifths of new supplies.[18] Instead of having first call over new supplies, monetary authorities are left with the residue after other demands have been met.

In the sense that the use of gold in industry and the arts has no direct monetary function—or at least is normally unrelated to speculation about the future price of gold in terms of different

[15] Samuel Montagu and Co. Ltd., *Annual Bullion Review*, London, 1951, pp. 3-5.
[16] W. J. Busschau, *Gold and International Liquidity*, Johannesburg, South African Institute of International Affairs, 1961, Table V, p. 72.
[17] Robert Triffin, *Gold and the Dollar Crisis*, New Haven, Yale University Press, 1961, Table 10, p. 53.
[18] *Annual Report*, 1963, p. 172.

currencies—the demand stems from different motives than the desire to hold gold in either official or private hoards. The use of gold as a metal for actual consumption in fact varies considerably with changes in income levels and movements in its price, compared with gold substitutes. For example, over the five years to 1938 compared with a similar five-year period up to 1928, the industrial use of gold fell away by just two-thirds.[19] Such a drop in non-monetary usage not only indicates the effects of increased gold prices following the devaluations of the early thirties but also the restrictions upon demand, at least for decorative purposes, flowing from the severe reduction in personal incomes during the depression years.

More recently gold consumption for industrial and artistic purposes has been growing relatively rapidly. Estimates based on MacDougall's data covering the nine years from 1947 to 1955 show that the quantity of gold available for official reserves increased at an average rate of $3 \cdot 2$ per cent per annum over the period, and while the demand for private hoarding showed no significant trend ($+0 \cdot 06$ per cent per annum), the increase for industrial use and artistic purposes was $7 \cdot 3$ per cent each year.[20] With the price of gold constant at $35 an ounce in a world of rising prices and growing real incomes, the relative cheapening of the metal has certainly stimulated its non-monetary use.

The stimulus to greater consumption through favourable price and income movements has been supported by a growing technical appreciation of the characteristics of gold. In pre-war years the most important non-monetary outlet was in the jewellery industry and this was followed by dental uses. Although these two uses are probably still paramount, gold is being used to an increasing extent as a coating to provide protection against heat and corrosion for aircraft and earth satellites. High purity gold costing about $65 an ounce is employed in the fabrication of silicon transistors and diodes for use in computers, aircraft missiles and satellites.[21] The demand for gold in these and other more

[19] League of Nations, *International Currency Experience* (Ragnar Nurkse), Geneva, 1944, Appendix 1, p. 233.

[20] Sir Donald MacDougall, *The World Dollar Problem*, London, Macmillan, 1957, p. 546.

[21] U.S. Department of the Interior, *Minerals Year Book*, 1959, p. 504.

mundane industrial and scientific purposes results from the
unique qualities of the metal (either alone, or as alloys in association with the platinum groups of metals) which include a
superior malleability, ductility and resistance to both tarnish and
corrosion.[22]

In the United States particularly, the non-monetary usage of
gold has been growing extremely rapidly over recent years. From
a figure of $51 million in 1957, consumption increased to $64
million in 1958 and to an average of $100 million over the two
years ended 1961.[23] There has been some recovery from scrap,
but non-monetary consumption of gold in the United States is
currently about double domestic production. This state of affairs
has led American gold producers to claim they have been sub-
sidizing the non-monetary consumption of gold.[24]

The use of gold for industrial and artistic purposes is normally
considered a respectable feature of the market, while private
hoarding paradoxically is thought distasteful.[25] From a monetary
point of view official antipathy against individuals holding gold
is easily explained. Central banking opinion is that gold should
not be held privately because national reserves are insufficient
to allow a withdrawal from official stocks. The International
Monetary Fund has supported this view—but *without* admitting
a shortage of world liquidity—in successive annual reports including 1963. In 1961, for example, the Fund stated: 'The
diversion of gold to private holders is of great concern to the

[22] See E. W. Zimmerman, *World Resources and Industries*, New York,
Harper and Brothers, 1951, revised edition, p. 764: 'It is claimed that one
gram of gold can be drawn into a wire 1·5 miles long.'

[23] *Minerals Year Book*, 1961, p. 604.

[24] See Statement of D. McLaughlin, President, Homestake Mining Co.,
San Francisco, in *Hearings Before a Sub-committee of U.S. Senate*, Government Printing Office, Washington, 1954, p. 271.

[25] The purchase of wheat or zinc—or even gold shares—against a suspected
subsequent price rise is not considered a vice. Gold itself is differentiated
and treated separately. In a rather narrow sense narcotics and gold can
be coupled, the private possession of either being illegal in some countries.
But the right to buy and sell gold is considered to be one of the most
important aspects of the gold specie standard, and the unfettered individual
right to trade in gold would be a step towards what many consider to be
sound monetary principles. So on one side the private holding of gold is
considered shocking, while on the other the view is that the state of affairs
will be shocking until people are able to trade in gold without legal
restraint!

monetary authorities of the world. Even with the improvements that have taken place in the reserve strength of many countries, it is still in the best interests of Fund members that, as far as possible, gold should be channelled into official reserves rather than into private hoards. Only as gold is held in official reserves can it be used by monetary authorities to maintain stability of exchange rates and to meet balance of payments needs.'[26] This is an official way of saying that, at the current price, gold is too scarce to be wasted in indulging the whims of private ownership.

Nevertheless the ownership of gold coins is tolerated in many countries. In the post-war period 20 franc gold Napoleons have been minted in France since 1951; Britain has minted sovereigns for overseas buyers since 1957 and South Africa began minting a two rand piece in 1962. Most coins are traded for their numismatic value, normally at premium prices, and since they are a relic of the gold standard existing before 1914 their possession frequently evokes a wistful memory of the good things of the past.

The hoarding of gold bars is of much greater importance quantitatively, and private trading in them is likely to continue so long as there are doubts about exchange values and gold prices. At any point of time the market for gold bars can be quickly stimulated by a suspected currency devaluation. For this reason it is difficult to make forecasts about the future private off-take. It depends partly upon how and when the monetary authorities will reduce or remove uncertainties about the price of gold in terms of national currencies, and partly on the capacity of governments to limit private buying. Currently it is possible to purchase gold bars in a variety of markets, but London is nowadays the major trading centre.[27] Gold bars of a standard size of 400 ounces (12·5 kilograms), normally costing about $14,250, are the usual transaction units in London and other Western European markets.

In addition to generally limiting supplies available for official hoarding, private speculators can cause further trouble because

[26] International Monetary Fund, *Annual Report*, 1961, p. 127.
[27] See Franz Pick, *Gold, and how and where to buy it and hold it*, New York, 1961, p. 38. On 16 January 1961 United States citizens' hitherto legal right to trade in gold bars on foreign markets was removed.

their peaks of activity occur during periods of financial strain. As the price of gold rises, doubts about the key currency component of reserves increase progressively, for at these crucial points of time the value of dollars and sterling is depreciating in terms of gold. The speculative process may therefore feed upon itself to an extent out of all proportion to the scale of the original disturbance. A cumulative buying spree on the London market in 1960 illustrated this point when gold sales reached a peak of about $40 on 20 October.

The Bank of England subsequently made arrangements with other central banks—and particularly the Federal Reserve—for sufficient gold to meet the market at these times, and with the aim of stopping such a speculative scramble for supplies. Thus the price of gold in London no longer reflects the extent of private demand. This has the advantage of easing each individual crisis and promoting general stability, but it also means that private holders can obtain a greater quantity of gold for the same cash outlay if an eventual price rise is considered likely. It may also involve individual central banks in a dangerous loss of gold while supporting other currencies. For individuals in many countries the private hoarding attraction of gold is not necessarily associated with views about its future dollar price, but instead is related to the exchange rate of the national currency against the dollar. Mr. Franz Pick in an intriguing book emphasizes this point in a list called a "currency cemetery". Over the twelve years from January 1949 to December 1960 the currencies of no less than sixty-nine countries have been buried there, having died from devaluation.[28]

In summary, gold has one great monetary advantage: it is generally acceptable, and its consequent assured convertibility into all other currencies makes it a more highly respected reserve medium than any national monetary obligation. One of the reasons for its continued monetary acceptability relates to the scarcity of the element; it cannot be "debased" by being artificially produced, and if gold is hidden away in abundance within the earth's surface, then it largely eludes geologists. At the same time the paucity of gold has also created considerable monetary

---

[28] *ibid.* (No mention is made of possible resurrection through subsequent appreciation!)

problems, and this has been a difficulty traversing centuries rather than decades. In certain respects, however, the twentieth century has produced new problems. Not only has the process of economic growth made the ready balancing of international payments more problematical, but the price of the metal has remained reasonably constant while inflation has raised commodity prices in terms of national currencies by multiples.

CHAPTER II

WITHOUT THE GOLD STANDARD
BETWEEN THE WARS

The progress of the political and economic system that had developed so strongly in the later nineteenth century was finally shattered by the first world war. A new technology was on the march during the war, and the close of 1918 not only saw the United States as a great new industrial power but all Europeans anxious to forget the calamity and its implications. At the end of hostilities, and before the reaction of disillusion became a force in the affairs of men, the major aim was to seek a re-establishment of the proven traditions set aside during hostilities.

The pure gold standard was included among the good things of pre-1914 which at the time were assumed to fit automatically all economic and political conditions, and at the end of hostilities the near single-minded aim of monetary authorities in Europe and North America was to return to the pre-war standard. Nor is this type of approach particularly extraordinary, for following the dislocation caused by any war the initial objective is concentrated on restoring the pre-war environment. Monetary authorities in this respect are no different from the great body of mankind in learning only slowly the consequences of war: on armistice day the victors are truly victorious and it may take several years or decades before the illusions of grandeur are finally set to rest by the implications of a new technology and of a changed political map.

Between 1914 and 1918 there was a great reshuffling of foreign-owned wealth. The United Kingdom reduced its capital credits by approximately $4 billion, much of this in sales of U.S. railroad securities to U.S. investors. France sold approximately $700 million of its foreign securities, but lost more than $4 billion of its investments in Central and Eastern Europe. Germany lost the bulk of its foreign investments, and the United States became the major international creditor.'[1]

A study of the inter-war period and its changed economic base from 1913 remains instructive to a world which is still learning some of the economic and monetary lessons of the first world war as well as those of the second. Even after half a century, preconceived ideas about what are considered to be the virtues of the pure gold standard still exert a strong restraining influence, not only in preventing the use of gold to best advantage but also in hindering the evolution towards more adequate international monetary arrangements. Partly because of the confusion between the concept of the gold standard and the concept of gold as international money, the objectives of world monetary policy have all too frequently remained clouded in uncertainties and doubts.

As the international monetary mechanism still requires adaptation to the situation arising out of the economic and political events of the twentieth century, a clearer picture of the present-day problems can emerge through a brief look at the fundamental politico-economic changes wrought by the first world war. The monetary machinery should always be made appropriate to the economic environment, not the other way round. The traditional school supporting a return to the gold standard would seem to have been out of step on this matter, for in their endeavours to change the economic realities since the first war by switching the machinery, means and ends have become confused.

At the risk of some repetition, the fundamental international monetary changes resulting from the 1914-18 war can be classified under four headings.[2] First, until 1913 England was the major centre for both short- and long-term credit and alterations in the short-term rate of interest were unnecessary to restrain undesired "hot money" movements. Owing to the pull of London there was no need to attract short-term capital by manipulating

[1] Raymond F. Mikesell (ed.), *U.S. Private and Government Investment Abroad*, Oregon University, 1962, p. 26.
[2] See W. A. Brown, *op. cit.*, Chapter 21, *passim*.

interest rates. In contrast to more recent years, the Bank rate in Britain could be made to conform with both domestic needs and balance of payments requirements. Then secondly—and again in contrast to the contemporary situation—London was the centre of the world's remittance mechanism, and both tradition and time gave a value to sterling equal to that of gold.

Thirdly, as mentioned in Chapter I, the British market set the level of world prices for most agricultural products. Incomes and prices in most outlying countries therefore tended to move with changes in British prices, and the resulting co-ordination made it relatively easy to keep the balance of payments in equilibrium and the exchange rates stable in creditor countries such as Britain. This complementary picture was completely distorted by the war, and the greater subsequent imbalance in net payments between countries gave an urgent priority to creating higher reserve levels.

The fourth great change also required the provision of increased quantities of international money. Prior to 1913 an extension of credit and loans facilitated an increase in export production within borrowing countries. Capital flows could be readily serviced, for the relationship between the financial and commodity aspects of international trade was reasonably harmonious. But since the first world war this pattern of specialization has been impaired and long-term capital flows have often disrupted rather than smoothed international accounts. Private capital has tended to move to deficit countries for the establishment of subsidiary plants and markets rather than for the financing of exports from them. In more recent years a multiplication of the numbers of separate countries plus great non-commercial transfers for military or humanitarian reasons have so distorted the pre-1914 capital picture that it is nowadays practically unrecognizable.

In the early twenties many of these changes had not gone very far in the light of subsequent developments, but nevertheless even then the dislocation put a strong premium upon the possession of gold. A solution to the developing scarcity provided by a new international currency or an increase in the price of gold was not even seriously considered at the time—nor is this surprising. All was automatically expected to return to "normal" with the rates of exchange coming back to pre-1914 parities. Tradition set the pace, and tradition was based on the gold standard system of the nineteenth century and on a deeply ingrained banking ethic—namely, that the pound sterling was an obligation to pay a certain weight of gold and that this obligation had to be maintained.[3] In the circumstances the monetary authorities faced an enigma. It was necessary to find more international liquidity to meet the requirements of a changed world system where some events like the Russian revolution had destroyed faith in many paper obligations and added to the scramble for the safe refuge ensured by the possession of gold. But no short-cut techniques such as a general revaluation of national currencies against gold or the establishment of a world central bank were allowed.

EXPERIMENTING WITH A GOLD SUBSTITUTE

Many countries responded to the need to increase their own international reserves by withdrawing gold from internal circulation. Between 1913 and 1925 no less than $2·7 billion worth of gold was released for international purposes by this technique.[4] Hence one of the principal methods of exchanging national currencies across national boundaries disappeared as gold was completely divorced from private trading transactions.

The international effort to find a solution to the shortage of gold culminated in the Genoa Conference of 1922 when the gold exchange standard was endorsed as the appropriate method of meeting the liquidity needs of a reserve-hungry world. Although gold was still at the centre of the international payments system the subsidiary changes were quite radical. Gold was no longer in use as national money, and national paper money obligations were to be used as international reserve money. Not only had gold vacated the domestic scene entirely but it also had to share the international arena with newly promoted national obligations.

The Genoa Conference in other words marked the arrival of the key currency principle, where nations held national money

---

[3] Brown, *ibid.*, p. 169.
[4] *International Currency Experience, op. cit.*, p. 7.

assets, in addition to gold, as buffers against changes in their balance of payments. During the nineteenth century gold had been supplemented with sterling, but at that time sterling was held for facilitating trade rather than for reserve purposes. The key currency principle was quite different and, as with gold, the key currencies needed to be both widely acceptable and unlikely to depreciate in terms of one another or against gold. The key currency countries also needed appropriate banking facilities where a growing volume of foreign-owned short-term obligations (the key currency component of reserves) could be satisfactorily traded. Only the United Kingdom and the United States had sufficient standing in international trade and banking to meet these requirements. They also seemed less concerned at the growing accumulation of their short-term I.O.U's by other countries, which were convertible into gold at the current rate of exchange.

One of the great problems with the gold exchange standard —and perhaps overlooked by its architects at Genoa—is that dollars and sterling can only be accumulated as reserves if America and Britain themselves run balance of payments deficits. The key currency component of reserves represents the difference between total receipts and expenditure on all international transactions. Under the gold exchange system, therefore, any additions to the total of international liquidity depend upon the fortuitous circumstances of the American and British balance of payments. Since the fluctuations in world gold mining output have tended to be less erratic than the net balance of payments position of the United States and the United Kingdom, this new technique of aligning the world supply of liquidity with world needs could scarcely be called an improvement on the old methods.

At the same time it was particularly important for Britain to retain the prestige and standing of sterling, for there was always the danger that foreign holders of the United Kingdom's short-term liabilities would transfer their affections to dollars or to gold. The only course through which the implied gold guarantee of sterling key currency liabilities could be maintained was for the United Kingdom to return to the gold standard (the gold bullion standard) at the pre-1914 rate of exchange.

But British prices were no longer so competitive as in pre-1914, and the way back to the parity ideal was through long and continued deflation. From early in the post-war period deflation was the official policy, but it rested partly on the hope that it could be limited by a price rise in America which would restore the British competitive position in external trade. As a result of the war the United States had a large gold hoard, and according to the accepted monetary theory this should have raised prices. In the event, United States prices remained steady during the twenties[5] and when Britain returned to the gold standard (the gold bullion standard) at the pre-war parity in 1925 it was necessary to continue the deflationary policies in the United Kingdom. In spite of the resulting dislocation and unemployment—which reached an ugly political and economic culmination in the General Strike of 1926—the balance of payments remained in difficulties, for British imports were surprisingly high in the latter twenties. The domestic stagnation and unfavourable exchange rates, furthermore, adversely affected British exports, and with the United Kingdom share of world manufacturing exports falling from over 30 per cent in 1913 to 23 per cent in 1929, it was unique amongst the industrialized countries of the world in experiencing a contraction in its volume of overseas sales.[6]

It was difficult for Britain to maintain its traditional role of supplying developmental capital to the primary exporting countries. For one thing, a capital outflow from a key currency country in balance of payments difficulties has the habit of flowing back in the form of a rise in its short-term liabilities. But the long-term capital outflow did not have the same self-equilibrating tendency apparent before 1914, for Britain was no longer the cheapest and most convenient market in which to spend the proceeds of British loans.[7] In other words, new capital exports from the United Kingdom did not do much to stimulate British exports and thus hold in check an uncomfortable build-up of short-term sterling owned abroad.

[5] F. C. Mills, *Economic Tendencies in the United States*, [New York], National Bureau of Economic Research Inc., 1932, p. 322.

[6] A. Maizels, *Industrial Growth and World Trade*, Cambridge University Press, 1963, pp. 189, 435.

[7] Brown, *op. cit.*, p. 616.

The initiative passed to the United States. The volume of American manufacturing exports more than doubled between 1913 and 1929 and its share of the world's total manufacturing trade increased from 13 per cent to 21 per cent.[8] Over the five years to 1929 the British net capital outflow had declined to average about 37 per cent of the pre-1914 outflow and was less than half the United States figure.[9] The system had changed from a gold and sterling exchange standard to one which included the emergent financial centre of New York, and other centres such as Paris, at times yielding dominant but unstable power.

In 1928 the French monetary system was re-established on the gold standard, and in an application of the rules according to the theory, gold only was acceptable in settlement of an enormous surplus which had arisen from the repatriation of capital and a current surplus in the balance of payments. The movement of gold to Paris caused an outflow from London and New York, which in turn not only put pressure on the dollar and sterling but also diverted the movement of capital towards France instead of to the traditional borrowing countries. The French gold imports aggravated the already strong pressure towards deflation in many other countries and especially Britain.[10] At much the same time the growing New York stock market boom attracted funds to the United States, so London in effect was caught between two strong magnets.

The attractions of the New York and Paris investment opportunities brought to an end the tendency for international capital movements to equalize international interest rates and instead forced a competitive raising of central bank interest rates quite contrary to the pre-1914 gold standard theory. In the circumstances the *de facto* co-operation between the centre creditor countries broke down and '. . . finally violated the first principle of any stable gold standard system . . . that there must be stable credit conditions at the centre'.[11] Instead of long-term capital flowing in the traditional manner from those in credit to

8 Maizels, *ibid.*
9 Mikesell, *op. cit.*, p. 36 ff.
10 *International Currency Experience, op. cit.*, p. 39.
11 Brown, *op. cit.*, p. 823.

those in deficit, the New York stock market boom of 1928-29 diverted capital to the United States from other creditor nations. At the same time the United States long-term capital outflow fell away for the same reasons and in 1929 was only one-fifth of the 1927 net outflow.[12] The international monetary system was not being lubricated, and the outlying and debtor countries had to adjust themselves to the best of their ability to the stresses and strains developing at the centre.

Even before these difficulties at the nucleus, the potential need for long-term capital in the twenties far exceeded expectations. Outside the industrial creditor countries this growing deficiency emerged quite rapidly and in some respects the primary exporting countries experienced the first visible shocks resulting from the return to "normality". As their expanded output coincided with the recovery of European agricultural production from 1925 onwards, export prices of many primary products began to fall. The decline in agricultural prices and the resultant changes in the terms of trade involved some primary exporting countries in severe payments crises. Responding to the difficulty in obtaining foreign exchange, Argentina and Australia were the first countries to refuse to exchange their currencies into gold at a fixed price as required in the restored gold standard. In itself this may not have been an important factor but other influences were at work which further magnified the world problems.

In the twenties, as in subsequent decades, the export of long-term capital from the centre countries was vital not only to the growth of world trade but also for any increase in the exchange component of the gold exchange standard. Capital exported by the United States allowed other countries to finance their imports. The cessation of this capital outflow resulted in a tremendous flurry with the primary exporting countries trying to maintain their overseas receipts for income purposes, and also to service debts from abroad. The debtor countries were in trouble on at least two counts in the late twenties. Firstly, the markets open to their exports contracted as tariff protected production in Europe helped ease the world prices of primary products. Secondly, at the same time as export income fell in

[12] *ibid.*, p. 812.

periphery countries, so too did the amount of capital made available from the centre. To the extent that overseas earnings or borrowing could no longer finance imports into the debtor countries, international trade in manufactures also fell, adding particularly to Britain's balance of payments problems.

The course of the world depression developed in separate stages. The early events occurred with the fall in export prices and the tapering off of support from the inherently weak international monetary system. The second stage—which pushed the depression into an unprecedented period of severity—was related to the external effects of the American collapse introduced by the stock market crash of 1929 and followed by a banking breakdown in 1932-33. This in turn further reduced demand for the products of the slowly recovering economies in the rest of the world.

In attempting to determine the onset of the depression, a League of Nations study suggested: 'The principal changes in trade balances . . . began in 1931, and it is customary to attribute them to the general rise in trade barriers from the latter half of that year. This increase in barriers, however, was itself clearly caused by the general nervous urge to achieve liquidity in international accounts, resulting from heavy capital withdrawals and known as the financial crisis of 1931. These capital withdrawals, in their turn, marked the climax of disturbances in the international capital and money markets that can be traced back to the middle of 1928.'[13] In other words, the weaknesses of the gold exchange standard acted as a primer for world depression.

Instead of funds flowing towards the countries with large short-term obligations, during critical periods the tendency was for the gold exchange standard to work in reverse. Once capital was withdrawn, confidence in exchange rates—the stabilizing factor in key currency reserves—was destroyed. In London the scramble out of sterling and into gold became unbearable, for following the initial movement of funds to New York and Paris, the resultant decline in United Kingdom reserves made sterling look progressively more uninviting. By 1931, and in the wake of a banking crisis in Germany and Austria, the United Kingdom was unable to recall sufficient long-term funds borrowed

[13] League of Nations, *The Network of World Trade*, Geneva, 1942, p. 93.

C

abroad to boost its dwindling gold stocks. The fallibility of borrowing short while lending long was again demonstrated—or, for that matter, of lending short in the support of others, for about £70 million in British short-term assets became frozen with the German bank closure of mid-1931.

In two months alone, £200 million of foreign-owned funds were withdrawn from the London markets.[14] In September 1931, when the Bank of England was forced to suspend automatic convertibility between gold and sterling, only £130 million of gold remained—insufficient to meet the sight liabilities which were being hastily realized. Sterling depreciated against gold by over 48 per cent in the next two months. Those external holders of sterling as key currency reserves who had not converted it into gold before Britain left the gold standard were in a difficult position. Just at a time when reserves were needed as a buffer against further shocks, their sterling reserves fell in terms of other currencies, causing a capital loss which itself sometimes made devaluation inevitable.

The first experimental approach to a gold exchange standard ended in collapse. As the possibility of capital losses from depreciating exchange rendered the holding of foreign balances extremely risky, the breakdown of sterling led in turn to a further scramble for gold through the liquidation of previously accumulated foreign exchange reserves. In the twenties the granting of credits by London and New York had supplied the debtor countries with a large part of their key currency reserves. The withdrawal of these credits in the early thirties tended to wipe out those same reserves. As debtor countries consumed their foreign exchange reserves for repayments to the key currency countries, it was not simply a transfer of international currency reserves, but a complete extinction of them. To quote Nurkse: 'The breakdown of the gold exchange standard involved a sharp reduction in the aggregate of international currency reserves not only through the *conversion* of exchange reserves into gold but also through the *absorption* of exchange reserves by payments to the reserve centres.'[15]

[14] L. Waight, *History of the Exchange Equalization Account*, Cambridge University Press, 1939, p. 6.
[15] *International Currency Experience*, *op. cit.*, p. 41 (author's italics).

26

TABLE 2

Central Banks' Foreign Exchange and Gold Reserves

(End 1928 to 1932 in $ million)

	1928	1929	1930	1931	1932
6 Creditor Countries:					
Foreign Exchange	1878	1604	1679	1024	348
Gold	1987	2430	2943	4214	4872
Total	3865	4034	4622	5238	5220
% Foreign Exchange	49	40	36	20	7
18 Debtor Countries:					
Foreign Exchange	642	688	621	192	157
Gold	1503	1411	1373	1059	1007
Total	2145	2099	1994	1251	1164
% Foreign Exchange	30	33	31	15	13

Source: International Currency Experience, op. cit., p. 41.

Figures in Table 2 show the course of events over the crucial years. Collectively the debtor countries began to lose reserves in 1929 and by 1931 this reached an unprecedented flood. Although the debtor countries tried to keep their gold stocks intact, in four years from 1928 they nevertheless lost nearly half their total reserves. The creditor countries actually gained in total reserves in spite of a near complete extinction of exchange as reserves. At the end of 1932 six creditor countries held over four-fifths of the world's supply of liquidity.

The remarkable changes which Table 2 depicts were not caused by a break with gold but through a collapse of the gold exchange standard. Indeed, disillusionment about the key currency segment and the liquidation of this exchange (which in turn added again to disillusionment) represented a flight to gold rather than away from it. Brown summarized the situation clearly when he wrote: 'Because of the profound influence of the [first world] war upon the structure of the world's credit system and upon the economic environment in which it operated, 1914-19 was a period that marked the breakdown, rather than the suspension or modification, of the pre-war international gold standard system. Because these changes were fundamental and enduring, the hard test of experience proved that there was no true restoration of the system after the war, but merely experimentation with it to meet a series of emergency situations in the hope of gradually achieving a genuine return to "normal". This hope proved illusory and the experimentation itself left its own inheritance. Therefore, when England suspended the convertibility of sterling in 1931, the international gold standard as a world institution entered into an historical phase which must be described by a stronger word than breakdown. September 1931 marked the beginning of its disintegration. This emphasis is not brought out adequately by approaching the task of interpreting the meaning and describing the consequences of England's suspension of gold payments from the viewpoint of sterling depreciating "in gold". It was in protest against such an approach that J. M. Keynes uttered his famous *bon mot* that sterling had not left gold but gold had left sterling.'[16]

The economic history between the two world wars centres around the year 1931. That year is not at the middle of the inter-war period; nor does it mark any sudden deviation from the rapidly altering pattern of economic changes in the later twenties. But in the field of international monetary affairs 1931 represents the dividing line between the fantasies of the twenties and the disillusionments of the thirties. It signifies, too, a final fading of the old order of political behaviour; from that time onwards newly emerged political systems prevented any re-establishment of the pre-1914 approach to international affairs.

REACTIONS TO A COLLAPSED EXPERIMENT

The painful, lengthy and far-reaching adjustments to the monetary and economic disorder took place during the following decade. It is difficult to suggest which point of time, if any,

[16] Brown, *op. cit.*, p. 1052.

represented the beginning of effective reconstruction. Economic changes have so many non-economic side-effects. Even today it is difficult to be sure that all the politico-economic results of the depression years have yet worked themselves out.

The reaction of individual countries to a discredited gold exchange standard occurred after 1931, with unco-ordinated attempts at achieving insulation from the world depression. This was attempted with the aid of such devices as drastically increased tariff protection, exchange control and currency depreciation, import controls and barter agreements, and new political systems which ultimately became the most significant and destructive development of the period. All the countries of the world joined in the unprecedented wave of exchange devaluation, except Germany and a few nations in Eastern Europe, where stern exchange controls were used instead.

The analysis becomes somewhat more complicated by the events from 1932 onwards, when the formal breaking up of even the modified gold exchange standard system produced at least three areas of influence—the world of the dollar, the world of gold, and the world of sterling. The residual effects of this rearrangement in trading and political alignments are much more important nowadays than the longer-term influences of the devaluation cycle. The cycle, being practically universal, had very little overall influence upon the exchange relationships among the principal currencies. When the process concluded in 1936 with an agreement between France, the United Kingdom and the United States to cease competitive devaluation, the relative exchange rates were not widely different from what they had been in 1930.

In a sense, then, the offsetting devaluations were a waste of effort. But one thing was very different, and that was the price of gold valued in terms of the devalued currencies. By 1937 the price of gold in terms of national currencies had increased by 70 per cent on the average.[17] If the time-sequence of the devaluation cycle had been compressed, then the "successive" downward revision of national currency values would have been replaced by an "all-round" revaluation of gold. That the increased price

[17] *International Currency Experience, op. cit.,* p. 132.

of gold averaged 70 per cent rather than 100 per cent or some other figure was due to fortuitous circumstances. It was certainly not determined by a carefully planned assessment of the world's requirements. A measure of this lack of caution—as against too much caution before the breakdown—is thrown into perspective by the United States devaluation of 1934. The United States dollar, unlike sterling, was not devalued under the pressure of external forces on an insecure gold base. Its gold value was reduced as an attempt to help relieve the desperate financial and economic conditions facing the new Roosevelt Administration which assumed office in March 1933.

The dollar exchange rate moved erratically in the early thirties while other countries were trying to adjust their economies to the changes in their balance of payments. The United States was losing gold in sudden withdrawals, although in several cases the trend was quickly reversed. The Administration was concerned with the political emphasis placed on the international stability of the dollar. It became essential that the external irregularities which largely came from staying on the gold standard should be replaced before the internal difficulties could be tackled, for the opposition parties criticizing the New Deal re-financing programmes were able to point to the lack of confidence in the American dollar. At the same time "staying on the gold standard" and maintaining the existing parity with gold were considered essential for the continued prestige of the dollar. In the circumstances some policy decision was required and President Roosevelt announced the new gold policy for the United States on 22 October 1933 in a radio broadcast. In one famous passage he stated: 'Our dollar is now altogether too greatly influenced by the accidents of international trade, by the internal policies of other nations and by political disturbances in other continents. Therefore the United States must take firmly in its own hands the control of the gold value of our dollar. . . . As a further effective means to this end, I am going to establish a government market for gold in the United States.'[18]

At the same time the new Roosevelt Administration attempted

[18] *Federal Reserve Bulletin,* November 1933, p. 699.

to stimulate the economy by increasing the level of prices. An old but nevertheless continuingly persuasive idea that the price level moves directly with the price of gold seems to have been resurrected and for a short period the dollar price of gold was periodically manipulated. The reasoning was apparently based on the depressed farming incomes, for according to Brown the object of the new gold price policy was to raise farm export prices by forcing a still further depreciation of the dollar in the foreign exchange markets. In other words, the aim was a competitive devaluation of the dollar.

In a proclamation on 31 January 1934 the gold content of the dollar was finally reduced to 59·06 per cent of its former parity (that is, a devaluation of about 40 per cent) and stabilized at an official price of $35 an ounce.[19] This meant that the American devaluation was illusory, for the average world depreciation against gold was 70 per cent, not 40 per cent. With the all-round revaluation of gold, the dollar therefore appreciated in terms of other national currencies. It is generally agreed that in forcing this alteration Roosevelt was mainly prompted by the advice of Professors George F. Warren and Frank A. Pearson, of Cornell University.[20] The subsequent rise in the United States price level was primarily due to measures of the New Deal and some fortuitous limitations on agricultural production imposed by drought. 'It is doubtful whether the abandonment of the

[19] The President's power to devalue the dollar further (to 50 per cent of its former parity) expired in 1943. Only an Act of Congress can now alter the gold content of the dollar. However, the market price for gold could be altered by a change in the buying policy of the Secretary of the Treasury under the Gold Reserve Act. But this would appear to be circumscribed by I.M.F. obligations, for under the Bretton Woods Agreement Act, 1945, any change in the par value of the United States dollar requires legislative action by Congress. (See M. A. Kriz, "Gold in World Monetary Affairs Today", *Political Science Quarterly*, December 1960, p. 504.)

[20] Cf. Charles O. Hardy, *The Warren-Pearson Price Theory*, Brookings Institution, Washington, 1935. Professor Warren was an adviser to the Administration in 1933 and the Warren-Pearson doctrine was based on statistical compilations and historical narrative rather than economic reasoning. Henderson was certainly inclined to this view when he wrote: 'This policy, adopted in the face of the vast American gold reserves, was something entirely new in monetary history . . . as it seems to have been largely inspired by a crude statistical generalization to the effect that the price level varied proportionately to the price of gold.' (Sir Hubert D. Henderson, *The Inter-war Years*, Oxford University Press, 1955, p. 258.)

gold standard and the gold purchase policy in fact raised prices by a single cent.'[21]

Nor did the increased price of gold in terms of national currencies stimulate the world economy. For one thing too much had happened by then and international confidence remained shattered. Even Keynes's *General Theory* of 1936 arrived far too late to influence official thought on deficit expenditure. At this stage economic solutions were outweighed by the challenges contained in the new political systems emerging in Europe.

The international financial system was operating in reverse. Not only had international capital ceased to flow towards the deficit areas; it was in fact being continually repatriated from them. In every year between 1931 and 1937 the debtor countries of the world lost capital.[22] Capital resources continued to flow towards the creditor countries and particularly the United States. Over the five years from 1933 America received as much capital as it had made available to the rest of the world over the whole period from 1921 to 1934.[23] Confidence in traditional capital flows could not be restored, for as war clouds gathered in Europe and exchange speculation became widespread, there was a huge movement of hot money in the form of gold towards the "deposit compelling" attractions of the United States. Over the ten-year period from 1929 the American share of the world stock of gold rose from 38 per cent of the total at the beginning to 71 per cent at the end.[24]

This last episode of the pre-war gold narrative demonstrates one factor very clearly: when monetary confidence was further undermined with the development of acute political pressures, gold was able to facilitate the movement of flight money—and especially since the higher price of $35 an ounce, plus additional supplies from new discoveries in South Africa, put less strain

---

[21] H. W. Arndt, *The Economic Lessons of the Nineteen Thirties*, London, Oxford University Press, 1949, pp. 38-9. See also Seymour Harris, *Exchange Depreciation: Its Theory and Its History, 1931-35*, Cambridge University Press, 1936, and the Brookings Institution study: *The Recovery Problem in the U.S.*, Washington, 1936, for a detailed account of the confusions of theory and practice in the depression period.

[22] Mikesell, *op. cit.*, p. 43.

[23] *ibid.*, p. 40.

[24] League of Nations, *Statistical Yearbook*, 1939-40.

on the quantity available for transfer. Obviously, *without* the revision in the price of gold resulting from the devaluation cycle, this huge hot money transfer in the last years of the thirties would have further crippled the foreign exchange system. But it did little or nothing to facilitate trade and in 1937 world trade was still down by one-quarter compared with 1929.[25] Each nation was still treating its economic wounds in isolation.

Although no reading of the events surrounding the 1934 dollar devaluation can discern a soundly based economic theory behind the action, and in spite of the proposals of the Warren-Pearson group of commodity-price manipulators, it is possible that some needs were met by that action, however imperfectly understood. After the dollar devaluation of 1934 and up to the outbreak of hostilities, the United States supplied the rest of the world with a large proportion of its international financial needs in the form of dollars paid out for gold. Prior to the depression years of the thirties, dollars were largely made available in the form of international loans. Although it was not an entirely satisfactory substitute, the swapping of gold for dollar credits at a price of $35 an ounce rather than $20·67 at least acted as a source of strength by making more international transfers possible for a given movement of gold.

The harvest of President Roosevelt's action in 1934 was not reaped until after the second world war. Americans during the late thirties were puzzled by the arrival and interment of so much gold in United States soil. But this very same gold, for all its maldistribution in the early years after the 1939-45 war, did mean that the United States was able to shoulder huge post-war reconstruction liabilities without concern for the level of reserves.

It would be a mistake to assume that the economic disasters of the inter-war years were not attended by efforts at international collaboration. Conferences on many aspects of the international economy occurred frequently after the end of the 1914-18 war. Most early discussion was associated with the problems of German reparations. The decline in international trade, however, prompted more strenuous international efforts

[25] Maizels, *op. cit.*, p. 427.

to prevent the disintegration of the trading and monetary system.[26] These efforts fell short of success because the problems were never stated with sufficient clarity, or detached from the special national interests involved.

The World Economic Conferences of 1927, 1930, 1931 and 1933 tried to establish some form of agreement about trade, international indebtedness and price levels, and an attempt was made to establish an international central bank (eventually emerging as the Bank for International Settlements). But to confront problems of such magnitude with national interests pulling in all directions imposed an impossible climate for satisfactory negotiations.[27] The experiences of nations during the inter-war period left enduring impressions. After the round of devaluations there was no solution in an alteration of par values as a means of establishing competitive price levels. Nor could the international monetary system be freed from dependence upon the dollar, for what remained of trade was largely sustained by dollar sources. No other currency could challenge the deposit-compelling power of the American monetary system, although several were adequate for the restricted trading areas they covered.

In 1918 the United Kingdom was paramount—or, at least in theory. After 1931, and at least partly owing to British errors, the mantle passed to the United States. But owing to the American concentration on solving domestic economic problems on a largely isolationist basis, the transfer in fact meant that there was no single country exercising leadership in international financial and economic affairs. The second world war, by displacing the depression and shattering the isolation, finally clothed the United States in its new responsibilities.

[26] H. W. Arndt, *op. cit.*, pp. 232-3.
[27] See W. A. Lewis, *Economic Survey, 1919-1939*, London, George Allen and Unwin, 1949, pp. 65-8, for a summary of the way the problems were presented and the conflict of interests.

CHAPTER III

WITH THE INTER-WAR
MONETARY SYSTEM AFTER 1945

When the second world war finished, its ashes were scattered from Auschwitz to Hiroshima. But for some countries—and the United States most importantly—the horrors of war were visited only on its armed forces, and the rest of the population experienced the security of assured full employment for the first time in a decade or more. During the hostilities new and challenging production demands stimulated American technology as never before, and by the close of the Pacific war the United States was the undisputed world leader.

In contrast to the plans for reconstruction after 1918, a simple rehabilitation of the pre-war environment after the second world war was right out of the question, for this invited a return of economic and political turmoil. Most economists took the view that the depression had never been cured but merely absorbed —perhaps concealed—by the war, and this characteristic had a strong influence upon early post-war thinking. It was widely accepted that with the peace, nations would once more stagnate unless the Keynesian theories of employment (which had become much more accepted since their first impact in 1936) were grafted into the political apparatus. Although the full employment policies proclaimed by many Western governments appeared to seek an end to depression by tackling its effect rather than its cause, the concept itself highlighted other deficiencies in the world of international economics. For one thing the international monetary machinery needed to be improved to meet these employment aims—and especially as the idea of competitive exchange devaluations was ruled out as a satisfactory method of meeting domestic welfare objectives after the experience of the thirties.

The war itself produced many other changes in the politico-economic map. The old colonial system was in decay—not only had the traditional mercantile basis of trade largely broken up, but the early defeats of the allies in the war with Japan had destroyed the myth of the white man's supremacy. The Atlantic Charter, detailing the objectives of the allies, had called for Freedom from Want and with the stimulation of a now famous article published in 1943 by P. N. Rosenstein-Rodan, a new theory of development was evolving, expressly showing that there was no economic reason for supposing the mass of humanity should continue to live at or near starvation levels. But economic growth in the underdeveloped areas required the priming assistance of long-term capital in large amounts and even during hostilities it was realized that the traditional capital exporting countries of Europe would also need considerable capital to finance reconstruction. There was therefore a massive demand for capital—capital for reconstruction as well as growth—and the United States stood alone as the country capable of supplying the needs.

Before the war came to a close, Britain made a quite remarkable attempt at two conferences—one in Savannah and the other at Bretton Woods—to introduce a world central bank and a new international currency, *bancor*, to replace the gold exchange standard discredited during the inter-war years. The British plans put forward at the time with persuasion by Keynes met with a much more conservative approach from the side of the United States. America had no official negotiator of the stature of Keynes, and in any case the United States could see no particular merit in a change giving less utility to gold when they held seven-tenths of the world's stocks.[1] The United States was primarily interested in obtaining freer trade, but realized the achievement of this objective in the absence of radical plans depended upon reinstating sterling as an international medium

[1] In all discussions for improving the international monetary system, the country with the strongest relative reserve position normally takes the *status quo* attitude, thus suggesting, for all the historical evidence to the contrary, that the authorities expect the present situation to be permanent.

of exchange and the setting up of some machinery to give individual countries an opportunity of borrowing while in temporary balance of payments difficulties.

The compromise outcome was the International Monetary Fund, largely designed to ensure monetary stability once the post-war reconstruction had been completed, and the Anglo-American Financial Agreement, which opened a line of credit to Britain of $3·75 billion with the aim of facilitating the reconstruction. Some of the critics (and particularly Professor John H. Williams of Harvard University) felt that the International Monetary Fund would not work effectively until the major reconstruction problems, specifically those of Britain, had been solved.[2] Williams propounded the "key currency approach" which was designed primarily for the restoration of the pound sterling as an international currency and reserve medium alongside the dollar.[3] The object of the Anglo-American Agreement, therefore, was to restore sterling to convertibility—in effect to return the international machinery to the multilateral position of the mid-twenties. A first attempt at a return to sterling convertibility was made in July 1947, but after the American loan —originally planned to aid British reconstruction over years— had subsequently become exhausted in a matter of weeks, the United Kingdom had to revert quickly to stern import controls.

ECONOMIC PROBLEMS OF ADJUSTMENT

Events were to prove that a repair of the international monetary mechanism depended upon a prior re-establishment of Europe in a traditional creditor role. The reconstruction needed a much greater capital outlay than the earlier war-time forecasts had anticipated. Not only did Europe have poor harvests and very severe winters in 1946 and 1947, but the complementary economies of Eastern and Western Europe were separated when the iron curtain was established. On the other hand, prosperity prevailed in North America during hostilities

[2] Richard N. Gardner, *Sterling-Dollar Diplomacy*, Oxford, Clarendon Press, 1956, p. 132.
[3] Robert Triffin, *Europe and the Money Muddle*, New Haven, Yale University Press, 1957, p. 138.

and immediately after they ceased. Nowhere 'was productive capacity impaired by the war, and in the U.S.A. there was a vast increase in industrial output, with little or no decline in the production of civilian goods, a great increase in agricultural acreage, and a remarkable series of good harvests. Hence the goods which Europe so urgently needed, and which she could not produce for herself, were available from across the Atlantic, and the only problem was to find means to pay for them.'[4] There was a tremendous pressure on the world's capital resources at this time. The solution could only involve a transfer of wealth across to the war-destroyed areas.

Not only was America unique in having sufficient productive facilities to meet the demands, but also it had sufficient gold reserves to facilitate the huge transfers. Between 1937 and 1948 the United States reserves of gold practically doubled, and by the end of this period—as shown in Table 3—instead of owning about one-half of the world gold stocks as in 1937, the United States was the owner of practically three-quarters of the total. Meanwhile, gold reserves of other belligerent nations were slashed. In the same period, Britain's gold reserves dropped by over 60 per cent, French reserves fell to less than one-quarter on pre-war, while Dutch gold reserves suffered an even greater erosion. The combined gold stocks of the United Kingdom, France and the Netherlands in 1937 were over 30 per cent of the world total, while the collective holdings of the United States, Canada, the South American dollar countries and Switzerland equalled 57 per cent of all official holdings. By comparison the ownership of reserves in the early post-war years was most lop-sided. At the end of 1948 the United Kingdom, France and the Netherlands held only 7 per cent of official world gold reserves and the dollar countries plus Switzerland (i.e. the hard currency countries) possessed no less than 85 per cent of the total supply.

In 1947, and as Stalin's Russia flexed to pose a challenge, the United States approach changed dramatically from the dogmatism of Bretton Woods in a crash programme for recovery under the Marshall Plan. In one year alone the United States

[4] Brian Tew, *International Monetary Co-operation 1945-60*, London, Hutchinson, 1960, p. 156.

made available $6·8 billion net, this sum being equivalent to the total net outflow of capital on governmental account over the previous twenty-eight years from 1919.[5] In total it took no less than $28 billion—or $43 billion including military assistance —to secure the reconstruction of Europe,[6] and even if the new international organizations could have been utilized, the resources of the International Monetary Fund or the lending facilities of the International Bank were a pale shadow of these amounts.

The massive United States capital movements in the later forties and early fifties fitted the evolution of the world economy. Both directly and indirectly Marshall Aid and military procurement helped in the return to convertibility of currencies. Directly, the outpouring of dollar grants helped the recipients to rebuild their own shattered gold and dollar exchange reserves and, as shown in column 5 of Table 3, the net American share of world reserves started to fall away in 1949. At the time recipient countries were glad and anxious to hold dollars as official reserves, for not only were these dollars covered about four times by gold (column 4 of Table 3) but being interest-earning they were in effect "better than gold". But the indirect effects of recovery aid were more important than the extra reserves in the long run. With production capacity created anew, the recipient countries of Europe were soon able not only to replace with their own production goods hitherto imported from the United States but were able to compete with America on all world markets.

So long as the United States gold reserves were able to facilitate the transfer, the capital movements met both the political objectives of the cold war and the humanitarian objectives of assisting economic growth. But by the early fifties the great and decisive United States dynamism seemed to grow stale. Her assured world leadership faded with the war in Korea and the rise of McCarthy. The latter particularly made it difficult to introduce new ideas into practical politics, while the huge American loss of life in the stalemate Korean War caused a reaction leading to the policy in international affairs that con-

---

[5] Mikesell, *op. cit.*, p. 53.
[6] Thomas Balogh, *Unequal Partners*, Oxford, Basil Blackwell, 1963, Vol. 2, p. 11.

TABLE 3

The United States Reserves in a World Setting: 1922 to 1963

Year	Net Reserves* ($ billion)	U.S. Gold Reserves to World Gold Reserves (%)	U.S. Short-term Liabilities to U.S. Gold Reserves (%)	U.S. Net Reserves* to World Gold Reserves (%)
(1)	(2)	(3)	(4)	(5)
1922	4·2	42	29	30
1925	4·7	44	30	31
1926	4·2	45	39	27
1927	2·4	42	65	14
1928	2·0	38	68	12
1929	2·0	38	69	12
1930	3·2	38	55	17
1933	6·1	33	10	30
1934	7·6	37	8	34
1935	8·8	46	13	40
1936	9·8	50	14	43
1937	10·9	51	15	43
1938	12·4	56	15	48
1948	18·6	71	24	54
1949	18·6	70	24	53
1950	15·7	64	31	44
1951	15·2	64	34	43
1952	14·2	65	39	40
1953	12·1	61	45	33
1954	10·7	59	51	29
1955	10·0	58	54	27
1956	8·6	58	61	23
1957	9·3	59	59	24
1958	6·0	52	71	15
1959	3·3	48	83	8
1960	0·5	44	97	1
1961	—2·8	41	111	—4
1962	—3·8	39	124	—9
1963	—5·2	38	133	—12

* U.S. gold reserves less U.S. official and bankers' short-term liabilities to foreigners.

Sources: International Financial Statistics; I.M.F. *International Reserves and Liquidity*, 1958, p. 63; League of Nations, *International Currency Experience*, adapted as necessary for 1934 dollar devaluation.

tainment is enough—that the *status quo* can be maintained by such inducements as economic and military aid.

The United Kingdom also showed little initiative, but in this case the attitudes seem to have stemmed from reactions to the superhuman wartime efforts. Having declined a leading role in Europe early in the peace, the major post-war British international economic endeavour centred round a rehabilitation of sterling something like the attempts between the two wars. But in this case the rehabilitation needed to go much further, for besides having an export industry reduced to a mere shadow of the American giant, total British short-term liabilities had risen to many multiples of its short-term assets.

In the United Kingdom the aims of domestic policy had to play second fiddle to the demands of sterling as international money, but as this required deflation at home the policy was largely self-defeating, since other manufacturing exporting countries with more dynamic growth became increasingly competitive. In any case the rehabilitation of sterling was a massive undertaking. In 1938 sterling short-term liabilities held by other countries were equal to 95 per cent of Britain's own reserves—being equivalent in this respect, and as shown in Table 3, to the United States position in 1960. By 1947, on the other hand, the short-term liabilities of the United Kingdom exceeded its liquid international assets by the staggering ratio of seven to one—which in turn necessitated the freezing of most sterling held abroad.[7] Sterling certainly could play no part in adding to total international reserves and the currency's rehabilitation in effect required a reduction in the sterling key currency component of reserves.

Two years later, in 1949, total sterling liabilities caused less immediate worry. The deficit on current accounts with the United States continued to cause concern, however, and in contrast to the parity policy of the twenties (subsequently so discredited as to be a convenient scapegoat for ensuing disaster), sterling was devalued by 30 per cent. A large part of the world, including the sterling area, most of Europe and Canada, followed suit, to give an average devaluation against the U.S. dollar (and weighted according to the trade of each devaluing country with

[7] Tew, *op. cit.*, p. 180, n.3.

D

the U.S.) of approximately 13 per cent for the world as a whole.[8]

If the dollar gap with the United States was due to over-valued currencies in relation to the dollar, the 1949 spate of devaluations did little immediately to help—or at any rate, little to improve the trade balance of other countries with America (though it did check the large speculative movements of capital towards the dollar). In 1949 Europe was still largely shattered, so that it could scarcely increase the dollar value of its manu-factured exports. Nor did imports into the United States show sufficient change in volume to compensate for the lower dollar price, these being dependent upon movements in American income rather than import selling prices. In addition, within devaluing countries the already wide physical controls over imports made extra price deterrents from the changed rates of exchange somewhat redundant. In contrast to the twenties when a more realistic exchange rate would have helped British economic growth, this time additional economic recovery was necessary before the altered exchange rates could have their desired effect. Even the best monetary arrangements can only assist economic growth and welfare, they can never guarantee it.

The overall effect of the 1949 experiment was nevertheless quite different from the cycle of devaluations in the early thirties. The earlier process was essentially an alteration of all currencies against gold, with relative foreign exchange ratios at the end of the cycle bearing a close approximation to pre-devaluation parities. The 1949 devaluation represented instead a realignment of soft currencies against the values of hard currencies. The significant fact of the second devaluation from the point of view of international liquidity was that in terms of U.S. dollars there was no writing up of gold reserves in any part of the world. The change in values between the two key currencies of dollars and sterling had, moreover, a depressing effect upon the dollar value of reserves in those countries holding sterling as international liquidity. With the sterling exchange rate moving from $4·03 to the pound down to $2·80, it was necessary to write down the dollar value of sterling reserves by a similar amount—and their real value by a smaller amount. In terms of

[8] MacDougall, *op. cit.*, p. 289.

U.S. dollars, world foreign exchange reserves in 1948 were $13·7 billion, but by the end of 1949 they had fallen 24 per cent.[9] Gold-holding countries (including the United States) nevertheless made windfall gains; each ounce of gold could be used to buy more local currency in the devaluing countries and therefore had command over more goods and services.

The 1949 devaluation did have another side-effect which was probably not considered important at the time. Scant attention was paid to the effects of the devaluation upon gold prices and gold production in non-dollar areas. During the second world war gold production fell away, partly through a diversion of manpower to other activities. With a constant selling price, gold producers were also burdened with the full increase in production costs. By 1945 world gold output had contracted so severely that total production was only a little over half the amount of the 1940 peak year. The 1949 devaluations offset many of these cost-price effects by giving a proportional increase in the selling prices from gold mines, thereby stimulating an increase in production.[10] Thus although the trade advantages of the British devaluation proved disappointing, the stimulus to gold production in South Africa particularly contributed to improving the sterling area's accounts with the rest of the world. Sterling area annual gold production increased one-half over the ten years from 1948. The improved flow of new gold not only took some of the pressure off sterling, but each addition gave an improvement to the world total of liquidity and a better spread of ownership.

Other factors also helped in the general recovery. With the formation of the European Payments Union a further means was found of moving towards currency convertibility, while still rationing the use of gold and dollars. In fact, the European Payments Union proved an interesting and largely successful experiment in offsetting the $10 billion loss of gold and dollar

[9] As would be expected, the devaluations affected the dollar value of outer sterling area reserves more than any other country or group of countries. At the end of 1949 the *dollar value* of total gold and exchange reserves of outer sterling area countries fell 36 per cent compared with 1948.

[10] In the United States, where gold prices have been constant since the devaluation of 1934, production in 1962 was only 32 per cent of the quantity produced in 1940.

reserves—measured at constant prices—suffered by European countries since pre-war.[11] The Union worked on an overdraft principle, where member countries extended limited overdraft facilities in their own currencies and in return received overdraft rights.

The great flow of capital from the United States continued all through the fifties. Direct private investment by American corporations in Europe and Japan stimulated production in the countries concerned, while much of the American aid to underdeveloped countries was spent on goods manufactured outside of North America. The outflow of United States capital lubricated international trade as never before, with the net outflow in money terms over the ten years to 1955 being well over double the net outflow over all the inter-war years.[12] While world manufacturing production increased 40 per cent during the years from 1948-50 to 1954-56, world trade in manufactures increased by no less than two-thirds.[13]

Although the United States capital transfers plus renewed industrial competition from Continental Europe and Japan started to take its toll of American net reserves by the mid-fifties, the process nevertheless helped sterling (as a key currency) in a negative manner. With a diminishing gold cover, dollars instead of being better than gold changed more towards being merely "as good as gold". During any sterling crisis there was therefore less incentive to rush into dollars. In any case the International Monetary Fund stood by sterling at such times in massive short-term rescue operations, thus not only proving the worth of its existence but also relieving the international money market of tendencies to take precautionary action when the British balance of payments was in difficulties.[14] Sterling too has felt a discernible change in its international function. Outside the sterling

[11] Triffin, *Europe and the Money Muddle, op. cit.*, p. 201.
[12] Mikesell, *op. cit.*, p. 53.
[13] Maizels, *op. cit.*, p. 80.
[14] From the inception of the Fund through to June 1963 the gross drawing by member countries has been $7 billion. Of this sum no less than 34 per cent has covered transactions with the United Kingdom. The International Monetary Fund in this sense has made possible the reestablishment of sterling as a key currency, and in particular the support of over $1·5 billion in 1961 tempered a strong speculative attack against sterling which developed in the northern hemisphere summer of that year.

area the use of sterling as a basic form of reserves has been diminishing; over the post-war years it has been increasingly used for the financing of trade in association with the world-wide banking, insurance and shipping services supplied by Britain. The principal national money held as international reserves has now become the dollar, this therefore being the national currency most threatened by capital movements in times of international uncertainty.

Because of these factors, and even though the great redistribution of reserves between the United States and Western Europe tended to bypass Britain in the switching process across the Atlantic, sterling was able to move slowly towards convertibility. In December 1958 France devalued the franc by 17 per cent, and the Bank of France along with twelve other European central banks accepted the obligation to convert foreign-owned balances on demand. In post-war international monetary affairs this event was the big leap forward towards a truly multilateral system of payments. The acceptance of non-resident convertibility brought in its train a similar move in a variety of other countries, closely connected with one or more European countries or as members of a monetary group such as the sterling area.[15]

MONETARY PROBLEMS OF ADJUSTMENT

Although there was considerable satisfaction in monetary circles at the restoration of convertibility, it soon became apparent that rejoicing was premature. Although convertibility facilitated multilateral trade—so desirable from the economic point of view—it also brought several tough monetary problems. While international trade remained restricted, the monetary problems of convertibility were not particularly apparent; it was only when

[15] In February and March 1961 the following countries accepted convertibility obligations under Article VIII of the International Monetary Fund Charter: Belgium, France, Germany, Ireland, Italy, Luxemburg, the Netherlands, Peru, Sweden, the United Kingdom and Saudi Arabia. During 1962 Austria, Jamaica and Kuwait were added to the group. Other countries which had previously accepted obligations of Article VIII were Canada, Cuba, the Dominican Republic, El Salvador, Guatemala, Haiti, Honduras, Mexico, Panama and the United States.

trade became freer that many difficulties of the inter-war years again became apparent.

It is important therefore to place the dash to convertibility within a world-wide perspective, for only then can the picture of contemporary difficulties be seen in a long-term focus. The United Kingdom, for example, made the pound convertible for non-residents only fifteen months after going through one of its most serious exchange crises of the post-war period at the time of Suez. In the words of Katz, 'perhaps the major factor contributing to the improved payments position of European countries was the sharp decline in the prices of Europe's imports, especially of foodstuffs and raw materials, which occurred during 1957'.[16] One peg on which the convertibility success story has hung was thus the fact that the terms of trade between primary products and manufactures moved in favour of Europe. In itself this makes for a difficult situation, for it implies that if the terms of trade should swing back strongly towards the primary exporting countries convertibility may then be endangered.

The idea that the continuation of convertibility depends even partly on the terms of trade favouring the manufacturing creditor countries suggests the world is short of reserves. If this were not true the impact of a changed distribution of reserves between countries, itself normally forthcoming with a change in the terms of trade, would not reach such dimensions.[17] A large flow of capital to the underdeveloped countries—and to the borrowing nations of the world generally—would reduce the level of reserves in the lending countries, for capital transfers shift some reserves at least temporarily towards borrowers. But as this process is dangerous to convertibility and especially to those countries making the greater relative share available, it is likely to be resisted, even though, as shown in subsequent chapters, an ever-increasing flow of capital is necessary to lubricate the international economy and to stimulate economic growth. On this count convertibility can only be preserved at the price of stagna-

[16] Samuel I. Katz, *Sterling Speculation and European Convertibility: 1955-1958*, Essays in International Finance, No. 37, Princeton University, October 1961, p. 22.

[17] At June 1963 the countries of North America, Western Europe and Japan held four-fifths of the world's gold and exchange reserves and over nine-tenths of all gold reserves.

tion. Where overall world reserve levels are inadequate, a drying up of capital can also bring convertibility to an end, as in the inter-war years.

If the creditor countries agreed to share the capital transfers on the basis of some formula, the position may not improve much. For one thing there is the preliminary problem of agreeing on some formula—would it be based on national income, size of reserves, military commitments or, say, volume of trade? But more importantly, individual creditor countries can themselves experience remarkable changes in their balance of payments over quite short periods of time, and all capital exporting countries may not therefore be able to keep to a pre-determined formula even if agreement about one was possible.

Another long-term difficulty is also making itself apparent. Convertibility itself is largely a product of capital movements— in this case the huge United States outflow since the end of the second world war, which has had the effect both directly and indirectly of reducing the American net reserves to a negative amount (Table 3). America now faces major problems, for the reserves of other countries, so far as these consist of dollars, are no longer covered 100 per cent by gold. In a scramble to convert dollars into gold (the possibility of which is inherent in the nature of convertibility) those making up the tail end of the queue would merely find the "bank closed" sign facing them. For this reason—and in contrast to the mid-fifties when dollars were as good as gold, and even earlier in the post-war period when dollars were actually superior—gold nowadays is normally considered a safer reserve medium than dollars. The only way the United States can improve the gold cover in the existing monetary framework is for it to run a surplus in its balance of payments, for then it will recover some of the reserves it previously lost to Western Europe.

Yet even if the United States is successful, the process is self-defeating. A repatriation of dollars to America as other countries run deficits to accommodate the American surplus brings in its wake an extinction of international liquidity, with the United States share of the remaining total rising proportionately. For this reason an American surplus does not solve the world's monetary problems but simply changes them from concern about the future of the gold exchange standard to concern about the future of convertibility.

In recent years the aim has been to postpone the policy decision required in supplying a satisfactory answer to this dilemma. Instead the *status quo* has been buttressed. Multilateral agreements have been negotiated to protect the dollar against speculative attack. A "lenders' club" of richer nations has been grafted alongside the apparatus of the International Monetary Fund, and club members have agreed to lend one another reserves for limited periods if this is considered to serve the lenders' interests. The International Monetary Fund itself has been strengthened. In September 1959, for example, a scheme was adopted increasing all quotas by one-half. The United States has acted unilaterally to strengthen its currency internationally by seeking to stop the dollar drain inherent in a continuing deficit. Remedies have ranged all the way from restricting tourist expenditure abroad to curtailing capital exports. Thus the contemporary world aim would seem to be concerned with giving priority to the short-term problems and then worrying about the longer-term problem thrown up in the process.

Although such tactics are understandable, they may nevertheless fall short of being laudable. The ideal solution—the basic solution—is one which simultaneously solves both the problem of the dollar (the gold exchange standard issue) and the world liquidity problem (the total quantity and distribution of reserves issue). Those policies not fulfilling such a dual role can scarcely be classified as providing a fundamental solution.

The history of the last half-century shows grave economic problems have arisen because the international monetary machinery has been imperfect. Nor is this particularly surprising when it is remembered that since the breakdown of the gold standard, the politico-economic aspects of international affairs have become quite disjointed from the monetary characteristics. The world political and economic map is nowadays greatly changed compared with the picture prior to the first world war. The international monetary system has by contrast scarcely moved at all; a strong emotional yearning for the gold standard seems to have ensured that the mechanism remains as close as possible to the old self-regulatory system even though the environment making this at all possible has now changed out of recognition.

The high-tide of the gold standard was probably reached about 1880 or a decade or so afterwards. Since then there have been two catastrophic wars which have quickened the pace of change, including political and social change, and a technical revolution which has given rise to something quite new in the world's history—the age of high mass production and high mass consumption. Since 1880 the *volume* of world exports of manufactured goods has increased over eight times, much faster than the explosion in population growth, which only managed to double over the same period.[18] No longer is the world so neatly divided between manufacturing and primary producing countries, all operating in a relatively free trade environment. Nowadays every nation wants and seeks the high mass consumption rewards from a successful drive to industrialization.

The process of technical advance and industrial development has produced its share of balance of payments problems through changing both the form and complexion of international trade. At the turn of the century, for example, over 40 per cent of the world exports of manufactured goods were textile products and just over 11 per cent comprised transport equipment and machinery. By 1959, in contrast, the roles were completely and almost exactly reversed.[19] Individual countries have adjusted their economies to technical change to the best of their ability, while the rate of adaptation has had a strong influence upon their competitive trade positions in international markets and their balance of payments strength. At the end of the nineteenth century Japan enjoyed 1·5 per cent of the total world exports of manufactures, but by 1959 its share had grown to 6·6 per cent. Over the same period the United Kingdom balance of payments strength and the position of sterling slipped from a position when Britain enjoyed one-third of the world's export market for manufactures, to where its share was only 17 per cent.[20]

Somehow or other the international monetary mechanism has accommodated economic changes such as these even though—and in spite of not being altered conceptually—it lost the self-

18 Maizels, *op. cit.*, Table 4.1, p. 80.
19 *ibid.*, p. 163.
20 *ibid.*, p. 189.

regulating characteristics of reserve and capital movements with the demise of the gold standard. Prior to 1914 international flows of investment were more or less assured and self-equilibrating. Although this may not have always produced the ideal world economy from the welfare point of view, it at least lubricated the international monetary system. After the second world war the international emphasis by contrast was very strongly directed towards economic welfare and for a while this also improved the monetary mechanism. Finally the synchronization broke down, for although the outflow of American capital since 1945 has facilitated growth in world trade and income, with an imperfect monetary system the movement of resources reacted to produce a toxic effect in the form of the enfeebled dollar component of reserves.

The international monetary machinery will only function satisfactorily when it is in a position to permanently synchronize both the short- and long-term objectives of the international economy. Ever since 1918 a great proportion of all international financial efforts have been devoted to propping up the system as crisis after crisis has threatened to tear the structure down. Given the weakness, the remarkable feature of international monetary affairs over recent decades has been the resilience. Given the problems, the ingenuity of officials has lain in accomplishing so much while doing little that could be labelled controversial. But this approach also means that despite all the discussions and machinery for international co-operation, each country fundamentally still tries to seek economic salvation in isolation. Each of them attempts to obtain balance of payments surpluses and this is *arithmetically* impossible for all countries collectively. Such a state of affairs bears strange contrast to the sound defences erected against potential physical attack. If the free world understands the necessity for military forces to deter armed aggression, it is surely sensible to construct adequate reserves of liquidity so that economic defences may be ensured.

CHAPTER IV

THE FUNCTIONS OF INTERNATIONAL RESERVES

International trade is one way in which nations together can advance their economic wealth. Because gold is universally acceptable as a means of paying the net debts from one country to another, it facilitates international trade. If there was no such universally acceptable medium of exchange, central bankers in each country would be in quite a quandary about what to offer and what to accept in settlement of net international payments. Traders consequently would be unsure whether any payment they received from abroad in a foreign currency could in fact be sold to the domestic banking system for local money. There would therefore have to be exact balance between each country's sales and purchases, and multilateral trade—which is implied in the idea of currency convertibility—would prove distinctly difficult. In these circumstances international trade could not be conducted in terms of national currencies, and the interchange of goods and services over national boundaries might even have to be through barter arrangements. Even under the present monetary arrangements, barter, and its extension of bilateral trade agreements, may prove more advantageous than no trade for countries particularly short of international reserves and needing imports. With larger supplies of universally acceptable liquidity, the system can move further away from barter towards the complete freedom of multilateral trade. With a reasonable cover by way of reserves, the monetary authorities of a country do not find it necessary to keep exact balance between foreign receipts and foreign payments. The higher the level of reserves, the longer can a country finance a given imbalance between gross receipts and payments without having to take offsetting action which may restrict economic growth and welfare.

It is also possible to say that reserves are needed to facilitate changes in the economic framework—to supply the lubrication of a dynamic international economy. Such an interpretation of the function of reserves means that if there are but few fundamental economic changes, or if the changes are well co-ordinated, then there is a lesser need for them than when future economic prospects are uncertain. The historical evidence gives support to this interpretation. Prior to the first war the world had yet to experience the rigour of many subsequent political and economic eruptions and there was a reasonably good international balance in the flows of trade and capital. In 1913 international reserves were equal to 21 per cent of imports for the year, but there was less concern about the adequacy of reserves than in 1962, when reserves equalled 50 per cent of the world's import trade.

Textbooks give a slightly different interpretation again, suggesting that the motive behind the holding of reserves is to ensure equilibrium in the balance of payments at the "chosen" rate of exchange. But in one sense the balance of payments will always balance whatever the rate of exchange, while the desirable rate of exchange is itself a function of the balance of payments. Normally—and with reason—the whole topic at the textbook level seems a delirium since it suggests all will be balanced and in equilibrium if all is balanced. As with most "Alice in Wonderland" concepts, there can be little doubt about the verity of the subject even though proof is hard to obtain in a statistical sense.[1] But if the concept of equilibrium is set aside, it is possible to define the balance of payments like an ordinary business profit and loss account; both always balance simply because both are accounting terms. When a country shows a surplus in its balance

---

[1] An examination of different publications for data in given years normally shows disagreement by some billions of dollars about levels of world trade, reserves, etc. Similarly, when using different issues of the same publication, one constantly finds figures over a number of years being revised and frequently by some billions of dollars. This is all very frustrating and at such times one is forced to the conclusion that if statisticians can find and lose so much money with such indifference, then either there is no shortage of liquidity or the creation of additional liquidity will cause little difficulty.

of payments, this is balanced by what may broadly be termed lending abroad or an accumulation of reserves. Similarly, when there is a deficit in the balance of payments, the deficiency is offset by borrowing abroad or by using reserves. Any lack of balance between the total inward and outward payments with the rest of the world normally makes itself felt through a change in reserves. Yet if the monetary authorities are able to

TABLE 4

United Kingdom: Balance of Payments and Reserves:
1946-62

($ millions)

Year	Net Surplus (+) or Deficit (−) (1)	Special Payments Inward (+) Outward (−) (2)	Change in Reserves (3)	Official Reserves at end of Period (4)
1946	..	..	..	2697
1947	−4131	+3513	− 618	2079
1948	−1710	+1487	− 223	1856
1949	−1532	−1364	− 168	1688
1950	+ 805	+ 807	+1612	3300
1951	− 988	+ 23	− 965	2335
1952	− 736	+ 247	− 489	1846
1953	+ 546	+ 126	+ 672	2518
1954	+ 480	− 236	+ 244	2762
1955	− 575	− 67	− 642	2120
1956	− 626	+ 639	+ 13	2133
1957	− 419	+ 559	+ 140	2273
1958	+1005	− 209	+ 796	3069
1959	+ 449	− 782	− 333	2736
1960	+ 771	− 275	+ 496	3232
1961	− 841	+ 928	+ 87	3319
1962	+ 842	−1354	− 512	2807
TOTALS	−6660	+6770	+ 110	+ 110

Note: Special Payments (column 2) include American aid, other similar payments and credits and United Kingdom transactions with the I.M.F.

Source: Adapted from *The Banker*, July 1963, p. 512.

introduce compensatory capital flows, the alteration in reserve levels may not reflect the balance of payments surplus or deficit on current account. Any lack of balance is then at least partly disguised by a change in the composition of the balance sheet. Some of these characteristics are thrown into relief by a study of the United Kingdom and the United States balance of payments as shown in Tables 4 and 5. For both countries (and for all countries) the change in reserves or net indebtedness abroad accommodates the net surplus or deficit.

In 1947, for instance, the United Kingdom had a deficit of $4131 million in its overall payments with the rest of the world (Table 4, column 1), but special payments through loans from North America very largely counterbalanced this and reserves were only drawn down by $618 million. If assistance amounting to $3513 million had not been made available in that year, and assuming imports would not have then been of a different value, Britain would have lost all its reserves and still defaulted on over $2 billion in short-term claims. The United Kingdom position for 1959 is an interesting contrast to the situation twelve years earlier. In 1959 the British payments surplus on ordinary transactions was $449 million, but in that year repayments on previous borrowing (which had been incurred to maintain reasonable liquidity in the form of gold while keeping the balance of payments in order) equalled a total of $782 million. The net result was that reserves were drawn down by $333 million. An even flow of trade and payments between nations can therefore depend upon capital just as much as reserves; a flow of capital and a flow of reserves may be considered as substitutes for maintaining equilibrium in the balance of payments.

Over the post-war years the United States balance of payments shows some similarities and some contrasts with the United Kingdom. Both countries have run sizable deficits (column 1 of Tables 4 and 5) but in Britain's case special payments have been sufficient to mask a loss in liquidity and have in fact given a slight increase in reserves. For the United States a great proportion of the inflow of special payments has taken the form of short-term dollar liabilities—the key currency component of other countries' reserves. But in contrast to the United Kingdom these special payments were less than the sum of

TABLE 5

United States: Balance of Payments and Reserves:
1948-62

($ millions)

Year	Net Surplus (+) or Deficit (−) (1)	Special Payments* Inward (+) Outward (−) (2)	Change in Reserves (3)	Official Reserves at end of Period (4)
1948	..	..	..	24,399
1949	+ 175	− 11	+ 164	24,563
1950	−3580	+1837	−1743	22,820
1951	− 305	+ 358	+ 53	22,873
1952	−1046	+1425	+ 379	23,252
1953	−2152	+ 991	−1161	22,091
1954	−1550	+1252	− 298	21,793
1955	−1145	+1104	− 41	21,752
1956	− 935	+1241	+ 306	22,058
1957	+ 520	+ 279	+ 799	22,857
1958	−3529	+1254	−2275	20,582
1959	−3743	+2668	−1075	19,507
1960	−3881	+2179	−1702	17,805
1961	−2370	+1628	− 742	17,063
1962	−2186	+1279	− 907	16,156
TOTALS	−25,727	+17,484	−8243	−8243

* Change in I.M.F. position and liquid dollar liabilities held by foreigners.
Sources: Adapted from the Brookings Institution, *The United States Balance of Payments in 1968*, p. 10, and *International Financial Statistics*.

the post-war balance of payments deficits—so the United States also lost $8 billion in gold.[2]

[2] This does not imply a reduction of net U.S. assets. On the basis of the American balance of payments definition, only the costs of acquiring foreign assets are shown. Since the acquired assets are not posted to the credit side of the balance, the acquisition of foreign assets depresses the balance of payments until dividends or repayments cover the original outlay. (See Brookings Institution, *The United States Balance of Payments in 1968*, 1963, p. 3 ff.)

THE USE OF RESERVES

Changes in the level of liquid reserves represent the difference between receipts and payments on overseas account including capital movements. Countries keep reserves for the same
reason as individuals try to retain a credit balance at the local
bank. Individuals, corporations and countries are alike in being
unable to arrange an exact balance between their income and
their expenses, and may find that income has a greater degree
of variability than expenditure. It is particularly difficult to
forecast balance of payments trends. In a study written in
1960, MacDougall made the following important comment
after considering the potential trends in the United States
balance of payments: 'There is a strong human tendency to
assume that the balance of payments cannot change very much
from what it is at the moment. This may be due to natural
conservatism or perhaps to lack of imagination. In fact, it can
change very rapidly. The fundamental reason is, I suppose,
that it is a marginal part of a marginal part. The balance is a
marginal part of the total trade and the trade is in turn a
marginal part of national income. The present U.S. deficit is
of the order of 4 per cent of the turnover in her international
transactions. . . . This means that if, for example, there were
a 4 per cent change in receipts, and a 4 per cent change in
expenditure in the opposite direction, the deficit would be wiped
out or, alternatively, doubled.'[3]

A country therefore attempts to maintain satisfactory liquidity
in the form of reserves since this allows it to continue payments
even while receipts fluctuate. If receipts show a downward trend,
a hoard of reserves gives a chance to defer recourse to certain
unwelcome corrective policies such as deflation at home, devaluation or import restrictions. Without reserves the monetary
authorities cannot ride out a deficit and their hands are very
largely tied to the quickest acting corrective, which may not
be the most desirable from the welfare point of view. In turn,
this means that the purpose of holding reserves—as the very
name implies—is not to facilitate a constant deficit with other

[3] Sir Donald MacDougall, *The Dollar Problem: A Reappraisal*, Essays in
International Finance, Princeton University, No. 35, November 1960, p. 64.

countries, as those who argue against increasing total international reserve levels sometimes suggest. Naturally it is easier for a rich nation to maintain reserves than its poorer neighbours for reserves represent current consumption forgone. But in normal circumstances even poor countries are eager to have at least minimum reserves for the very sound reason of avoiding international bankruptcy in periods of stress.

More light can be thrown on the appropriate use of international liquidity by considering the functions of reserves more specifically. In subsequent chapters particularly it will be argued that reserves are needed to meet or facilitate changes in the economic framework—to smooth the problems associated with economic growth in other words. In the remaining pages of this chapter the aim is to show the monetary function of reserves by tracing the effects of some economic changes.

It is apparent that the value of exports of a particular country may be reduced for a variety of reasons. It could result from a technical break-through where a new synthetic at least partially replaces the "natural" product that was previously an important export; it could be because newly developing nations cut off other countries' traditional export markets through their own protected production; it could result from a general world down-turn in business.

This buffer function of international reserves can be made clear by a simple example.[4] Imagine a country—the home country —where the authorities are determined to maintain national income at levels consistent with adequate employment and existing wage rates. If for instance tariff protection in traditional overseas markets reduces exports, there will be a loss of income in the export industries.[5] If nothing is done, the loss of expenditure on home products through the depression in the export industries may yield cumulative deflation in the domestic indus-

[4] See Ragnar Nurkse, "Conditions of International Monetary Equilibrium" in *Readings in the Theory of International Trade*, London, George Allen and Unwin, 1953, p. 16 ff.

[5] If it is a manufacturing export country, there will also be a loss of employment in the export industries. If it is a primary exporting country, the immediate problem will normally be in the terms of trade rather than employment.

E

tries. To prevent the spread of deflation, the home country must endeavour to offset the decline in foreign purchases through maintaining domestic expenditure while altering the productive pattern of the economy should this be necessary. Although this policy of "offsetting" may maintain stability in the domestic economy, it gives instability to the balance of payments since imports then tend to remain up in the face of reduced exports. A country pursuing an offsetting policy must therefore be prepared to lose reserves temporarily—perhaps for several years—in order to meet the deficit and while seeking to develop new export markets and new export products. With the level of imports reasonably well maintained, the gap in the balance of payments will be greater than if deflation was allowed to spread through the home economy.

A further and salutary effect of such policies is that deflation in the home country is not then spread abroad. It can be said that such a policy—possible with reasonably large reserves—minimizes both the duration and intensity of recession periods. With insufficient reserves each country lacks a "buffer" to maintain imports when export receipts fall, and the mechanism for maintaining the balance of payments may instead have to be one of devaluation, import restriction or deflation.[6] Since these latter alternatives restrict imports, they have a cumulative effect upon the deflation abroad, and therefore upon world trade and the commodity terms of trade. Talk of international trade out-

[6] With convertibility the emphasis is towards deflation. But a change in the social arrangement of Western countries has narrowed the "deflatable" sector. Compared with earlier decades of this century a higher proportion of the total expenditure is governmental. An expanded share of the national income also goes to lower income groups. The effect of these changes has been to give much greater stability in effective demand, with the "deflatable" sector being more and more restricted to the durable consumer goods sector. Having to carry the whole burden of deflation the reduction in output in these industries may have to be severe periodically. The process itself gives political trouble in affluent democratic countries (the need to make do with less durables being just as aggravating to consumers as to producers). For these and other assorted reasons import restrictions are normally the first choice. With a lack of reserves and international pressure including International Monetary Fund pressure against physical controls, the durable consumer goods sector may expect to remain the victim of stop-go economic policies.

stripping the growth in world reserves does not make sense in this context. Ultimately there are either sufficient reserves for world trade at the level appropriate to reasonable employment levels and exchange rates, or the required restrictions and unemployment will reduce trade to levels compatible with the value and distribution of world reserves.

Another reason for holding reserves is to enable countries to withstand a temporary period of financial or physical crisis. Natural disasters can have a profound effect upon the balance of payments, causing imports to rise while exports may drop. In some countries the failure of a crop (e.g. coffee in Brazil) can produce severe drains on reserves, and even a strike (e.g. the United States steel strike) can have a similar influence. If reserve levels are inadequate, even a change in personal tastes may produce a balance of payments crisis. A good example is the rise in the United States demand for European cars prior to the introduction of the American compact. In this case the American compact car represented the United States adjustment while a sufficiency of reserves covered the interim.

Yet in normal circumstances most crises result from changes in the value of exports relative to the value of imports—to changes in the income terms of trade, in other words. Internationally traded goods can be separated into two broad categories of primary products and manufactured goods and their relative prices can fluctuate considerably. As individual countries tend to be either predominantly exporters of manufactures or exporters of primaries, so too does their balance of payments position alter with changes in the terms of trade even though the physical volumes traded could remain unchanged. In the contemporary world, furthermore, the terms of trade of an individual country may be strongly influenced by the process of technical and political change.

It may take years for a movement in the terms of trade—advantageous to one group of commodities and one type of country—to work itself into the other direction. If the change results from technical factors there may never be a return to pre-existing conditions. This means that in addition to having reserves for financing immediate short-falls (due, say, to a crop failure) the gigantic task of reserves—or capital movements—is to outlast swings in the terms of trade.[7]

With a reasonable buffer of reserves a country also finds it easier to maintain stability in the home economy without too much concern about the balance of payments. A summary of the detailed studies by Professor James Meade includes four fundamental combinations of internal and external economic conditions. These are set out in Table 6. In all these four combinations it may be necessary to use reserves while the economy is being stabilized. In conditions as shown in row 1 (inflation at home combined with an external deficit) reserves will fall until the appropriate remedies become effective. The remedies suggested for conditions of external surplus combined with deflation at home (row 2) will also reduce reserve levels. In certain circumstances the ability to reach satisfactory levels of employment in the home country will depend upon the absolute level of international reserves. If a country has the misfortune to experience deflation at home plus an export deficit (as shown in row 3) reserves will fall until economic readjustments take effect. When reserves are relatively high and the balance of payments is in surplus (suggested by row 4) then imports can be raised—perhaps by an appreciation—to check the inflation.

TABLE 6

Domestic and External Economic Conditions with Remedies

Conditions		Remedy
1. Inflation at home ..	External deficit	Cut spending High interest rates
2. Deflation at home ..	External surplus	Raise spending Low interest rates
3. Deflation at home ..	External deficit	Monetary "conflict" —devalue
4. Inflation at home ..	External surplus	Monetary "conflict" —revalue

Source: The Economist, 26 November 1960, p. 930.

[7] Generally speaking a country exporting and importing a good range of both primaries and manufactures has less need for reserves since price movements in one direction are counterbalanced by movements in the opposite direction.

RESERVES AND EXCHANGE RATES

If the overseas receipts of a country always equalled its overseas expenditure, there would of course be no real need for reserves. A technique for moving at least partially towards such a principle of policy is to use a system of flexible exchange rates in place of the present-day fixed parities held stable through buffer stocks of international liquidity. Instead of allowing reserves to fluctuate and so fill the gap left from movements between a short-fall or excess in the balance of payments, the exchange rate may instead fluctuate to equate, or attempt to equate, the supply and demand for foreign currencies. So far as this is done it is unnecessary to hold a buffer of liquidity, for the exchanges themselves move up and down adjusting current import demand to current export receipts. In the United States the flexible exchange rate idea finds strong support in what is known as the Chicago School approach and from time to time this view has received support from other groups, such as the Brookings Institution.[8]

Yet for a number of reasons freely floating exchanges have never been very popular in the world of commerce and politics. For one thing, the demand for imports in many countries is rather unresponsive to changes in external prices. This may occur in a variety of ways but normally it is associated with the difficulty of substituting domestic products for imported products.[9] The resulting import inelasticities mean that big changes are frequently required in currency values for small movements

---

[8] Actually the Brookings Institution idea is to utilize both flexible and fixed parities (see *The United States Balance of Payments in 1968*, p. 258 ff), but partly on the basis that if it is difficult to lift reserves then the need for them should be reduced. ('The great danger of a system of fixed exchange rates operating with the existing and foreseeable level of reserves is that it does not permit deficits to be financed long enough to make the kind of adjustments that are most often needed. Deflationary measures, the classical means of improving the balance of payments, cut employment and real incomes—effects which are neither politically feasible or socially desirable in a modern industrial country'. *ibid.*, p. 246.)

[9] For example, how does one substitute Australian petroleum for imported petroleum; United States "Scotch" for Scottish "Scotch"; Egyptian aeroplanes for United Kingdom aeroplanes; German tobacco for Virginian tobacco?

in trade. At the commercial level such variability in the rates of currency exchange are extremely frustrating to import-export business. Secondly, and because the role of exchange under the flexible system is established by supply and demand, an increase in the supply of the currency normally depresses its price. Capital transfers therefore become problematical. It is difficult to imagine an easy transfer of untied economic aid, for if a donor country gave more relatively then amongst the donor countries it would experience the greatest relative devaluation. In any case official support to smooth the market—which depends upon the use of reserves—could not be long lacking, for lumpy capital or trade payments and receipts would otherwise cause unnecessary fluctuations.

Although fully flexible exchanges without any price support are therefore unlikely, it would nevertheless be unwise to dismiss a partial movement towards flexible exchanges, obtainable by widening the maximum and minimum deviations from parity of individual currencies. If exchange rates were allowed to fluctuate a little more freely or if parity was not so rigidly pegged, the fluctuations in other things like reserve levels or the state of business activity might be a little less.

Instead of moving towards greater flexibility governments will probably continue to be reluctant about making even occasional alterations in par values. They are tied, rather loosely in actual effectiveness, to the objectives of the International Monetary Fund, which require an agreement on generally fixed exchange rates. The primary objective of the International Monetary Fund is to maintain stable exchanges. Other factors are probably still influential, and Katz summarized a number of them well when he wrote: 'Because government officials have been conscious of the political consequences of exchange-rate actions, exchange-rate policy has often been dominated by domestic political, rather than economic or financial, considerations. Devaluation has usually been resisted because it was a public admission of mismanagement, or at least it provided political opponents with the grounds for making such a charge. On the other hand, appreciation has been resisted because the voices of those hurt by appreciation have been loud. . . . With conflicting interests involved, government officials have been tempted to avoid any change in exchange rates and thereby avoid the cross-currents of criticism which any change in par values would entail.'[10]

With alterations in the rate of exchange being therefore in the category of "action of the last resort", the holding of reserves is likely to remain as the cornerstone of the international monetary system. Even then the use of reserves is not appropriate to meeting all deficits in international payments. The use of reserves typically fits those deficits which in a broad sense are fairly quickly self-liquidating. Such "temporary" deficits may arise from a short-term outflow of liquid capital, a drought in a primary exporting country or a widespread strike. But in a world of change, the balance of payments problems of a country all too frequently result from more fundamental causes. A deficit in a country may occur at the same time as a low rate of growth compared with its international competitors, for faster growing countries are normally more competitive in price and product development. Whatever the original cause, a country in this position may suffer prolonged difficulties. Devaluation— even if this is possible in the political sense—may not in any case be effective and if reserves are not at the optimum level, internal deflation to preserve the balance of payments may add to the relative stagnation. In these circumstances and as depicted by the American assisted recovery of Western Europe and Japan after 1945, an inward flow of capital is the appropriate method for resolving the problem. Table 4, showing Britain's post-war balance of payments, is a good illustration of the accounting.

The level of reserves in most countries is insufficient to finance some transactions. Individuals do not normally purchase houses for cash, and all but the richest corporations are unable to finance their development from their own resources. Similarly most countries are dependent upon outside capital to assist in their drive to industrialization. The use of reserves can normally cover only those quickly reversed abnormalities whose effects may or should only last two or three years at the most. Few countries can afford to accumulate reserves to meet all potential needs, and even if they are rich enough, such a policy in a

[10] Samuel I. Katz, *op. cit.*, p. 27.

world of restricted reserve creation means they must run a balance of payments surplus and reduce the reserve levels of other countries. The use of reserves may therefore not be appropriate for meeting abnormalities lasting longer than just a few years. For example, the balance of payments of a country may take five to ten years or more to recover from a technical breakthrough which has the effect of severely reducing the value of its exports. An inward flow of capital, besides minimizing the loss of reserves, might also help to adjust the economy to the changed conditions.

Thus although capital flows and the use of reserves have different functions (or should have different functions), they are similar in that they help to maintain order in the balance of payments during a process of readjustment. With an easy flow of long-term capital round the world it is less necessary to try and use reserves for facilitating changes of a longer-term structural nature. Any shortage of reserves is then less apparent. Alternatively, if the flow of capital slackens off, the need for reserves increases proportionately. If the flow of capital slackens because a shortage of reserves makes its ready transfer difficult, then the international monetary system is in a precarious condition, for the lack of the one leads to an increase in the needs for the other. Countries individually may seek to counter an imperfect flow of capital or a paucity of reserves by increasing exports, for a balance of payments surplus is an obvious way of building up reserves. Another method of helping to maintain or augment reserves is to restrict imports, and one of the most absurd aspects of the international economy is the sight of practically all countries seeking to maximize exports and minimize imports. World exports equal world imports, so that considered collectively the sum total of these policies is to reduce world trade. When all else is said and done, therefore, one of the basic functions of reserves is to facilitate the easy flow of international trade.

In summary then, each country seeks to keep reserves for a variety of reasons, but they are all centred around giving freedom in national economic policies while maintaining balance in international payments. Since the aim of national policies is normally to maximize rates of economic growth, the supply of a

easonable level of reserves to the world with a satisfactory dis-
ribution can have an ironic feature. In these ideal circumstances
here is less need for individual countries to apply trade reducing
medicine and the need for reserves to cover the range of
exigencies mentioned in this chapter is proportionately reduced
-the exigencies themselves being less likely to arise. Alterna-
ively, it is possible to suggest that a shortage of reserves soon
becomes apparent to all but the few surplus countries, for
he functions of reserves in most nations then have to cover a
wider range of tasks. In turn this means it is difficult to assess
he need for reserves objectively, for at any time it depends
upon such things as the flows of world trade, the movement
of capital between nations and the health of the international
monetary machinery. A further consideration of these factors is
herefore needed to arrive at even subjective conclusions about
he desirable level of world reserves.

CHAPTER V

INTERNATIONAL LIQUIDITY FOR TECHNOLOGICAL CHANGE

The danger is ever present that some careless action will spark off world calamity. The threat of great devastation from total war nowadays hangs over mankind. But the potential for doing something silly is not restricted to the purely political arena and the action—or rather the lack of action—about vital economic issues could bring in its wake unnecessary hardships for the greater part of mankind. Indeed the international repercussions from a particular political course of action seem to be both well-known and appreciated, and this may in itself ensure an escape from total war. But on the side of economics the issues appear less understood, perhaps because they are less clear-cut. The diagnosis of particular economic problems is all too frequently incomplete or inappropriate, leading in turn to miscalculations about the scope and nature of the therapy needed.

The United States deficit provides a classic example of the way in which the elements of an economic problem may be examined in a context which merely adds to confusion rather than detracting from it. The Chairman of the Board of Governors of the Federal Reserve System did a service in placing the central issues of the American balance of payments into a meaningful position when he said: 'Our international payments deficit this year [1962] was less than one-half of 1 per cent of our gross national product. That deficit did not represent a decline in our international wealth because the rise in our foreign assets exceeded the drop in our net monetary reserves. Yet the deficit was of vital concern in that it extended by one more a series of large deficits, a series that has now persisted for five years.'[1] In turn such a diagnosis suggests a particular therapy: a therapy which enables the United States to continue its deficit until the previous capital outflow pays off on the income side. Since the diagnosis points to a greater lack of reserves compared to other variables such as income, any attempt to restrict income to fit the level of reserves seems a meaningless solution.

This example has a moral. A clear understanding of the functions of the international monetary system within the international economy is needed, for otherwise the diagnosis and therapy of economic and monetary ills could be misjudged. Not all of the world economic problems would nowadays seem to be placed in their correct perspective, and this can make technical difficulties look as though they are economic problems. In these circumstances, and instead of correcting the international machinery, the aim is to alter the international economy.

But as the international economy is actually altering and changing as a result of advancing technology and other influences, any pressure seeking to gain conformity to the needs of the international monetary system may not necessarily be in a direction which will allow economic progress to proceed smoothly. Technological change, for example, operates quite independently of the international monetary system, even though it influences world monetary requirements. On one side, the process of technical change gives rise not only to new products but also to the methods of producing them. On the other, it can alter living standards—possibly lowering them at least temporarily in areas adversely affected by the change, while raising them in others. Changing technology and income, the twin pillars of economic growth, therefore affect both supply and demand on a world-wide scale and can bring varied pressures to the balance of payments of individual countries. Once it is agreed that it is impossible to halt the process of change and economic development—even if this should be desirable—the course of action is clear. In these circumstances the needs of the international economy should dictate the monetary requirements and not the other way round.

[1] William McChesney Martin, Jr., "Monetary Policy and International Payments", *Journal of Finance,* Vol. XVIII, No. 1, March 1963, p. 5.

Such a statement is axiomatic and would not need to be stressed except for the fact that in the real world the functions of the international monetary system are often interpreted in a variety of ways. For example, central bankers may primarily look upon reserves as a means of securing the immediate payment of net international debts, while the economist may regard them primarily as a means for ensuring economic growth. These two rather different approaches give rise to conflicting statements concerning such matters as the adequacy of reserves. The misunderstanding is fundamental and unfortunate, for both characteristics are closely interrelated. Balance of payments problems may arise as a result of the process of technological change and economic growth, yielding a monetary reaction which may dampen the ability to invest in technological change and so check the rate of growth. In other words, if growing pains bring balance of payments difficulties, then the rate of growth may have to be held back to minimize them in the absence of adequate reserves.

There is a need to show the relationship between the international monetary system and the international economy, for only through such a study can the monetary requirements be at all accurately determined. Besides an assessment of the monetary needs of the gold exchange standard, the study calls for an analysis of the broad economic developments in the world as a whole. For this reason it is appropriate to look at some of these changes in the world environment to see how they affect the balance in trade and payments between countries and international monetary needs. These matters will be treated in the present and succeeding two chapters.

TRADE IN A CHANGING WORLD

Unless each nation lives out its destiny in economic isolation, a change in the economic climate in one country may concern other countries of the world in a variety of ways, and in turn produce different secondary reactions which may or may not compensate the original movement in the initiating country. As productivity increases (normally more quickly in the rich countries and more slowly in the poor) and population expands (normally more slowly in the rich countries and more quickly in the poor), the trading characteristics of nations and commodities making up this trade also undergo continuous alteration. Each change affects different countries in different ways, giving a large number of individual reactions. But concise study is not only complicated by the varied reactions. The international mechanism is especially complicated because instead of having one or two countries as necessarily favoured by many economic textbooks, the world total of countries and trust territories numbers just 200, and each is somewhat different in regard to total population, national income and stage of economic development —let alone such matters as relative dependence upon trade and the nature of its trade.

Therefore it is only possible to make a broad assessment of the effects of changes in the world economy and even then to generalize somewhat about the influences. But since the breakdown of the gold standard, sufficient changes have occurred in the international environment for it to be possible to predict the requirements of the international monetary system. Much has been covered in a descriptive sense in earlier chapters; here the aim is to examine the process of change so the monetary needs can be more readily estimated.

Any fundamental alteration in the characteristics of international trade is not only expressive of the nature of economic change, but also it points the way to the challenges faced by particular countries in adapting to the new conditions. On page 49 mention was made of the great twentieth century trade substitution in international transactions; textiles have declined to relative insignificance, while sales of machinery and transport equipment have grown from insignificance to predominance. With industry more widely spread than at the turn of the century, fewer textiles are traded, simply because more countries manufacture their own, and this creates problems for traditional exporters like Britain. The process works in the other direction for more intricate products produced by advanced methods. The demands for imported capital and transport equipment have risen in relative importance, for few countries are willing or able to enter the competition of making items like jet transport planes and heavy electrical equipment. Since the turn of the century, in fact, trade in capital goods has formed the most dynamic element of international business, doubling in volume every decade if the depression years are excluded, and favouring the balance of payments of those countries supplying the types of capital needed.[2] Oil too has rapidly increased its share of world trade and it is nowadays an essential commodity in all nations. The major exporters of such products are favoured. Conversely, in the many countries of the world without domestic supplies of basic commodities like oil, this characteristic of indispensability adds to the difficulties of lowering total imports by traditional techniques during periods of balance of payments stress.

Some countries are therefore relatively lucky, receiving the bounty of nature while others are less fortunate in this respect even though they may be bigger in terms of both area and population. The importance and scope of trade for each country consequently varies. Some nations may be in a position to supply those types of goods most demanded in world trade; others may be able to offer only those items more favoured by consumption patterns of a previous century. Some countries may be so well endowed by nature, or so well protected from competition—or perhaps so primitive—that international trade constitutes only a very small proportion of their transactions. In the United States foreign trade is equal to only about 7 per cent of national income but in Australia it is near 30 per cent. Because of the very size of its gross national product, however, the United States affects the rest of the world through its income fluctuations.[3] For instance, in 1964 the external trade of the United States represented 15 per cent of world trade while Australia's share was under 2 per cent. A recession in Australia therefore scarcely makes a ripple on international waters. The position of the United States is quite different, and because America is also a key currency country, it may well be uniquely different. Suppose the United States ran a balance of payments surplus through

[2] Maizels, *op. cit.*, p. 258.
[3] In 1961 the gross national product of all the countries of Western Europe was only two-thirds that of the United States (Brookings Institution, *op. cit.*, pp. 41, 44).

a recession at home. In this case not only does the volume of world trade shrink, and so endanger the growth of the world economy, but world reserves also decline at a most inauspicious period when the dollar component of reserves is progressively repatriated. Thus by its very nature economic change affects the commodity patterns of international trade, and in turn this can produce varied reactions in different countries, giving rise to yet further side-effects.

Rising living standards—the very essence of twentieth century economic change—can also create balance of payments problems directly. At each stage of growth, specific products can be identified as holding the major share of the extra consumer expenditure. For instance, as rising income in Western Europe increases the demand for durable consumer goods relative to items like foodstuffs and clothing, so too may the more efficient suppliers of durables like the United States perhaps sell more in that market, thus improving its relative balance of payments position.[4] Again, the balance of trade advantage between countries changes; in this case a short-run advantage accrues to one country as the productive process in others is adapted to new consumer requirements, possibly with the assistance of a capital inflow from the richest countries establishing subsidiary plants in these areas. In advanced countries with reasonable stocks of international liquidity, the balance of payments pressure from rising living standards may be short-lived, if it occurs at all. If the local population is sufficient to support domestic production of newer products, the productive capacity of the economy can be adapted to meet the new pattern of demand. On the other hand, if it is a relatively poor country—or such a small country that local production is unwarranted—the balance of payments pressure arising from a given increase in living standards will be more persistent and it could make further rises in living standards difficult.

Smaller or relatively poor countries normally seek to induce economic growth and lower the propensity to import by protecting local manufacturers through tariffs or other import-restricting devices. In turn this policy may stimulate an inflow of private capital which also helps to minimize any balance of payments

[4] The Brookings Institution, *op. cit.*, p. 54.

difficulties in the shorter run.[5] At the same time the drive to industrialization with the aid of protection helps to explain changes in the commodity patterns of trade. The volume of world trade in textiles has declined over the last half-century because these items are easy to make (and are in demand) during the early stages of industrial development. In such cases the adjustment is relayed back to the traditional exporting countries in the form of a worsening of the terms of trade, and the balance of payments could be under strain until new and more appropriate export markets are developed—or, in other words, until the commodity and income terms of trade are improved. Since the process may take many years, large reserves are needed to ensure a successful adaptation. Otherwise the need to restrict imports for balance of payments reasons could lead to relative stagnation, with the income terms of trade worsening rather than improving.

Indeed, the net balance between the net foreign receipts and expenditure of any country is strongly influenced by relative movements in import and export prices. The terms of trade in the contemporary world are of particular importance, for with a reluctance to cut employment levels in deficit periods and so much trade being taken by essential items like oil and capital goods, the volume of imports cannot change greatly in the short period. With a worsening of the terms of trade, rapid export stimulation—even if this were possible—may seem self-defeating in a price sense. The immediate reaction, in a world where exports cannot normally be increased at will, is to cut imports, and in turn this may develop a bias towards restricting imports more and more to "essential" items.[6]

In normal circumstances, and in the absence of equalizing capital flows, the total of net deficits and surpluses for the world as a whole grows larger if there is a marked change in the terms of trade between manufactured products and primary products. This results from the fact that most countries are predominantly exporters of one or the other group. Within the same group—

[5] See pages 85-6.

[6] After all, most countries tend to watch exports to see how much they can import rather than looking at imports to estimate how much needs to be exported.

he industrial countries, for example—the terms of trade may also change as factors like different rates of economic growth and technical innovation influence relative export prices for their own differing parcels of exports. Table 7 reflects the post-war position for a range of countries.

There are two points covered in Table 7. The last column shows the slowly worsening terms of trade position of the primary exporting countries (so far as the United Kingdom terms of trade can be taken as indicating the relationship between prices of manufactures and those of primary products) and the

TABLE 7

Percentage Shares of Gross World Reserves by Countries or Areas: selected years, 1948 to 1962

Year	United States	Sterling Area	Industrial Countries[1] Including U.S.A.	Industrial Countries[1] Excluding U.S.A.	Primary Exporting Countries[2]	Terms of Trade[3] (1948=100)
1948	50	19	65	15	35	100
1951	47	20	67	20	33	82
1954	41	20	69	28	31	94
1957	41	17	70	29	30	97
1960	30	17	71	42	29	105
1962	26	17	76	49	24	111
1963	25	..	71	46	29	..

Notes: [1] Industrial countries include Belgium-Luxemburg, France, West Germany, Italy, Netherlands, Norway, Sweden, Switzerland, United Kingdom, Canada, United States, Japan.
[2] I.M.F. member countries excluding industrial countries.
[3] United Kingdom (export prices divided by import prices).

Source: International Financial Statistics.

secular decline in the proportion of world reserves being held by this group. Even in 1951 during the Korean War boom, and when the terms of trade were distinctly favourable to the primary exporting countries, collectively they nevertheless showed little propensity to hoard reserves. In fact the countries of this group, including no less than fifty-six members of the International Monetary Fund, are normally always short of reserves in the sense that export earnings plus net long-term capital inflow

F

(but not short-term borrowing facilities) dictate the level of imports.

The second point from Table 7 concerns the industrial countries and the remarkable change in reserve holdings over the post-war period within this group of countries. In 1948 the industrial countries excluding the United States held 15 per cent of the world's gross reserves; in 1963 by contrast they owned nearly one-half of the total. Most of this improvement has been at the expense of America, and in general terms this kind of movement has a different influence upon the international economy from that caused by changes in the commodity terms of trade referred to above.

A switching of reserves between industrial countries has a less direct effect upon world trade than a change in the terms of trade between manufactured products and primary products. If there is a shortage of liquidity, a balanced distribution of reserves among the various industrial countries is more directly important for ensuring stability in the gold exchange standard and a continuation of the traditional flows of capital from the creditor industrial countries to the debtor primary producing countries. If there is a reasonably good distribution of reserves between the industrial countries and the rest of the world on one hand, and among the industrial countries themselves on the other, then the world economy is likely to be fairly tranquil. The great problem and danger of the present day is that the system is under strain at both of these points at the same time.

The dangers inherent when there are multiple pressures on the international monetary system are at least partly based on psychological considerations. If the flow of international trade and payments should stagnate, then business and commerce in trading nations become less optimistic and more cautious. In deflationary periods associated with a downswing in business activity it is difficult to moderate the general feeling of pessimism, while during an upswing it is sometimes difficult to dampen optimism about the future. In looking at the causes and consequences of the Wall Street boom of 1928-29 Galbraith wrote that 'speculation on a large scale requires a pervasive sense of confidence and opinion and conviction that ordinary people were meant to be rich'; and in the contrary situation, 'while people are cautious, questioning, misanthropic, suspicious, or mean, they are immune to speculative enthusiasms'.[7] The latter condition applies to recession. For this reason it is much easier, as modern governments have frequently discovered, to enter a state of deflation than to escape it.

A similar situation applies in international trade. During boom periods (the prevailing economic experience during most of the last decade and a half) reserves seem to be insufficient to service the desired level of international trade and payments. Trade normally increases more quickly than reserves. In more depressed periods, by contrast, the economic philosophy is reversed and individual countries tend to become more isolationist in their approach to international trade. Reserves then become an insulating factor against adverse world conditions rather than a means for facilitating international development. The level of reserves may grow more quickly than trade.

During depressed periods reserves must be proportionately higher than at normal times if they are to stimulate confidence, both internationally and internally. In a survey of these characteristics it has been suggested 'that reserve changes in the vicinity of the optimum are probably much less effective in time of slumps, when the optimum is high relative to the value of transactions, than in time of boom, when it is low'.[8] If additional reserves are to be created the ideal time to do this is therefore in more buoyant periods, and especially as a shortage or maldistribution of liquidity may otherwise induce a sharp business downturn. In boom periods, in fact, when confidence in trade expansion is high, the world may totter happily on the brink of crisis if reserves are below the optimum. From the strain on liquidity during the upswing of the trade cycle, a collapse of the system can set in motion not only a slump but it may also bring about the need for additional "insulation" reserves. As shown by the experience of the thirties, an increase of liquidity during depression does little to stimulate confidence. Indeed, in practically every adaptation to economic and technical change, whether in boom or depression, there is a need for liquidity.

[7] J. K. Galbraith, *The Great Crash*, 1929, Penguin Books, 1961, pp. 187-8.
[8] J. Marcus Fleming, "International Liquidity: Ends and Means", *I.M.F. Staff Papers*, Vol. III, No. 3, December 1961, p. 446.

A claim could be made that the world therefore has been short of reserves ever since the breakdown of the traditional gold standard, irrespective of whether sufficient funds have been available to service current rather than optimum levels of trade. Statistics showing the relationship between the value of gold reserves and world trade certainly highlight the situation. In 1913, for example, official gold reserves were only sufficient to finance world imports for a ten-week period. A careful reading of the economic literature of the period suggests little concern about the position.[9] By contrast, in 1938 the relationship between world trade and reserves was such that official gold stocks were enough to finance imports over a period exceeding fifty-seven weeks. Yet with the strain upon their liquidity during the depression, most countries of the world were in desperate need of additional gold to boost shaky reserve levels—as is indicated by the literature of the period. In 1964 reserves had shrunk so much in a relative sense that they could only cover world imports for twenty-four weeks. But objective judgments one way or another about the adequacy of reserves on this basis are impossible —for in addition to the changing environmental influences upon requirements, reserves in any case do not finance directly the total value of trade, but only the net debits and credits amongst countries (and even then only after capital movements and other flows have influenced the net balance).[10]

Other characteristics of the international economy support this contention, for if a country should seek to minimize reserve losses following an economic or technological change, the level of international trade itself may also become affected. For example, the domestic aim of richer countries in balance of payments

[9] As noted in previous chapters, the association between trade flows and capital movements was relatively well meshed before 1914. According to W. A. Brown, 'the elementary banking maxim that the more perfect the clearance the less the need for cash was exemplified on a world scale' (*op. cit.*, p. 787).

[10] To suggest a need for reserves by such a technique does not take account of influences arising from a change in the terms of trade. If, for example, the price of primary exports fell heavily, reducing the value of world trade, then the ratio analysis would imply an improved overall position just at a time when the balance of payments for many countries could be worsening, and when the total of net deficits and surpluses amongst countries would probably be increasing.

difficulties nowadays appears to centre around maintaining the social advantages of high employment. Wages are also normally inflexible downwards for welfare reasons. The level of reserves tends to run down while the productive process is altered, mainly in the direction of stimulating exports and replacing imports. The difficulty here is that such essentially long-term policies when combined with external convertibility may have little chance of being effective before reserves are exhausted—and especially when many countries adopt the same policies. In these circumstances the level and distribution of reserves greatly affect the rate of growth and levels of trade.

The system is further complicated if the levels of reserves do not err on the side of being more abundant rather than less so. Using a system of exchange and import controls, the world is never *really* short of liquidity. In these circumstances trade will be reduced to a level consistent with the current supply and distribution of reserves—any short-fall from optimum levels of trade and growth is held captive to reserve levels. With the system of convertibility, the process is largely geared the other way round, and any short-fall in optimum reserve levels is reflected in the problems associated with keeping international payments and trade flowing.

In the long run, reserve levels and trade come to a position of uneasy equilibrium. It is therefore difficult to accept the view that world liquidity should be increased only if the monetary growth in trade demonstrates the need. In these circumstances the only indication of a need for reserves would be in the difficulties of maintaining the gold exchange standard with fairly widespread convertibility of currencies. But undue concentration on this type of difficulty means that the direct emphasis is on averting a monetary breakdown rather than on directly facilitating growth in the world economy. Again, therefore, these considerations point to the need to make some distinction between the need for reserves to ensure continuing confidence in internationally used currencies, and the need for reserves to maintain adequate liquidity for ensuring an optimum growth in world trade and output. In the contemporary world the monetary needs are often taken as indicating total needs. This may be unfortunate, for an analysis within the broader framework could suggest a

greater need for reserves than many people may yet be prepared
to admit.

INTERNATIONAL RESERVES FOR A CHANGING WORLD

If an international monetary breakdown can be avoided, then
it may be expected that world trade will seek to expand over the
foreseeable future. Trade in manufactures alone should ensure
such a growth, even though the proportion of industrial goods
entering international markets over the last half-century has
been a declining proportion of all manufactured goods made
and consumed. Between 1913 and 1959 in the industrializing
countries the proportion of imported manufactures making up
consumption fell from 60 per cent at the beginning to only 18 per
cent at the end.[11] Nevertheless the imports of manufactures consumed by these countries rose by two-thirds over the forty-odd
years, because a seven-fold increase in total consumption more
than counterbalanced the declining proportion entering trade.
The same kind of thing happened in other groups of countries. In
industrial nations, although imports of manufactures supplied
only 4·4 per cent of the total consumption in 1959 compared with
8·4 per cent in 1913, the huge expansion in the very size of the
market caused the value of imports to double.[12] For this reason
world economic growth increases the need for trade. The only
sure way of keeping trade expansion in check is to restrict
growth.

The drive to industrialization in the less developed countries
will, if successful, do more than increase trade. It will also diver-
sify the world economy. Even now very few countries, if any, can
be classified as solely primary exporting or as exporters of manufactures. Most primary producing countries sell some manufactures and most industrial countries also export primary products.

[11] A. Maizels, "Recent Trends in World Trade", *International Trade
Theory in a Developing World* (Roy Harrod and D. C. Hague, eds),
London, Macmillan, 1963, Table VII, p. 50. (The countries include Aus-
tralia, New Zealand, Union of South Africa, India, Pakistan, Argentina,
Brazil, Chile, Colombia, Mexico, Turkey and Yugoslavia.)

[12] *ibid.*, Table X, p. 51. (The industrial countries are those countries
listed in Table 7, page 73.)

Although the export of manufactures from the primary producers in 1960 was 14 per cent of their total exports, these countries did not supply much of the world trade in manufactures—only 6 per cent, in fact.[13] The relative position for the manufacturing countries in 1960 was remarkably different. Not only were their exports of primary products near 30 per cent of their total exports, but the industrial countries supplied two-fifths of the total world's trade in primary products.[14] Exports from the richer industrial countries have been much more diversified. But their gain in this respect goes further, for the industrial countries have also expanded their exports of primary products much more quickly than have the traditional exporters of these products. In the fifties the industrial nations scored a 50 per cent increase for primary exports against a 25 per cent increase from the primary producers.

Thus there has been a relatively slow growth of exports from the primary producing countries and if this is not improved, then difficulties with their balance of payments, which have become apparent over the last decade, will continue. A change is unlikely in the foreseeable future according to Maizels, and for a variety of very sound reasons.[15] For one thing, the industrialization of primary producing countries has caused a sharp increase in their imports of capital goods and semi-manufactures. In marked contrast the policies of agricultural self-sufficiency in the industrial countries, instead of stimulating the international demand for primary products, have instead depressed it. Furthermore, in the industrial countries the balance of domestic demand has shifted towards the "growth sectors"—such as the chemical and engineering industries—and it is in these industries that the proportion of imported raw materials used per unit of output is normally much less than in the older industrial sectors like textiles and food processing.

Technical changes have further upset the traditional balance of the world economy, for in addition to turning demand away from many natural raw materials, they have in some cases gone

[13] Maizels, *Industrial Growth and World Trade, op. cit.*, Table 15.4, p. 393.
[14] *ibid.*
[15] *ibid.*, pp. 83, 84, 395 ff.

further through developing and producing alternatives in the form of synthetics. 'Synthetic detergents have made great inroads into the market for vegetable oils for soap; plastics have been substituted for non-ferrous metals, leather and other natural products; and synthetic fibres have displaced cotton and wool.'[16] This trend should continue to work against the older forms of primary exports, for in an era of scientific revolution, technological innovation may well accelerate. Protection policies within industrial countries reinforce these trends. Tariffs on raw materials like wool and cotton not only keep prices received by producers at a discount, but stimulate the substitution of synthetics for the natural product by raising their cost to consumers.

There would appear to be no quick solution, for these changes in the trade relationships between the industrial countries and the primary producers are largely of an organizational nature and inevitable in a world of rapid technical change. Indeed, and for the reasons outlined above, further technical advance is likely to increase the imbalance between the two great groups of countries. Nevertheless technological advance also offers hope for a longer-term solution. Sooner or later the process of change, through making countries more similar, should bring a greater degree of equilibrium. Successful economic development implies and necessitates a movement away from concentrating production upon goods no longer in high international demand. The drive to industrialization, if successful, is therefore the impetus that may bring balance once again to the world system of international payments. This means that solutions to international trade difficulties cannot be found in simple recipes such as a return to the gold standard. Whatever the international monetary system, the lack of balance will probably widen over the next decade or more, until the drive to industrialization in the present primary producing countries makes the world more evenly industrialized.

The great international economic challenge is therefore twofold. Firstly, there is a need to find an immediate means of bringing a greater degree of equilibrium between the collectively richer industrial countries and the collectively poorer primary

16 *ibid.*, pp. 395-6.

producers. The second requirement is to ensure that the means justify the end: that the balancing of international trade and payments should be by a method which promotes the successful economic development of the poorer nations. In turn the dual needs are largely associated with an inflow of capital, for it is unlikely that the export earnings of the primary producing countries will be sufficient to promote a quick rise in living standards.

In fact, the export problems of the primary exporting countries have increased considerably since the end of the second world war. Up until then trade between the two groups of countries was more evenly balanced. An expansionary influence in the industrial nations tended to raise the world demand for foodstuffs and raw materials. In such periods of general expansion the supplies of primary products normally increased more slowly than manufactures, so that with growing demand for both kinds of goods, the price advantage tended to turn towards the primary products as their supply was more restricted. The commodity terms of trade, in other words, turned in favour of primary products in the expansionary phase of the trade cycle. But since the end of the second world war the situation has changed. The industrial nations have gained both in volume and price because a relative expansion in the share of world trade represented by manufactures has not caused a counterbalancing movement in the relative price in favour of primary products. It can be expected that these trends will continue, for they spring specifically from the influences of the changing technology mentioned above and are supplemented by the protectionist policies of industrial countries. Although reduced barriers to trade would help ease the lack of balance between the two groups of countries, they cannot fully offset the effects of technical change on the demand for many primary exports.

In one sense, then, technological advance has made it difficult for the poorer countries to advance technically. Such a situation benefits no country in the free world. Although the 28 per cent of the world's population living in North America, Western Europe and Japan consume about 82 per cent of *all* production of non-food manufactures, no less than 45 per cent of the world's exports of manufactures go to the primary producing countries.[17] Owing to the economic interdependence between the two groups of countries, undue restriction on imports for balance of payments reasons can make growth in all countries more difficult.

The residual solution is a movement of capital from the surplus industrial countries to compensate for the export disadvantages caused by technological change and agricultural protection policies. The analysis therefore suggests that the solution lies in what was also one leg of the traditional gold standard. If such a response is not forthcoming, then the drive to industrialization will be held in check by balance of payments difficulties, in turn prolonging the imbalance in international accounts between the richer industrial countries and the collectively poorer primary producers. But, in contrast to the gold standard theory, there is nothing automatic about such capital movements and particularly at the amounts needed.[18] According to Maizels, the total capital requirements of the primary exporting countries could grow from the level of about $7 billion annually in the late fifties up to approximately $18 billion *net* by 1970-75.[19] This matter will be treated at some length in the next chapter. The essential point, however, suggested by the analysis is that reserves must be adequate, for if the industrial countries feel insecure with existing levels of liquidity, then the temporary loss of reserves associated with a flow of capital may well make it practically impossible for them to supply capital flows at this level or even on a much smaller scale.

It is difficult to estimate the exact level of reserves needed to facilitate a more even balance in the world economy over the next decade or two. Even in a perfect international monetary environment the structural changes following from technological change normally cause at least temporary difficulties for some countries or some individuals. But in a world with less than per-

[17] *ibid.*, p. 11. For all industrial countries taken together, 11 per cent of all manufactures produced were exported in 1959. But except for the United States the proportion was much higher. In France 18 per cent of total manufacturing was exported; for West Germany 23 per cent; for the United Kingdom 19 per cent; for Canada 14 per cent; for Japan 23 per cent and for the United States, 4 per cent. In this context world stagnation may help the United States balance of payments.

[18] See pages 84-5.

[19] *ibid.*, p. 19.

fect international monetary machinery, the needed capital flow may not be forthcoming, with the result that a favourable adaptation to change becomes increasingly difficult, if not impossible. One of the great practical problems about ensuring that sufficient reserves are available to make capital transfers relatively easy is that few countries appear willing or anxious while in surplus to admit faults in the monetary system and they usually decry the notion that any shortage of international liquidity exists. The net effect is to throw back upon the semi-chronic deficit areas the responsibility for all adjustments. In other words, those countries in a position to make possible any adequate international monetary reform will generally consider reserves to be ample unless the balances of some of these countries with each other—of which the United States deficit is an example—should reach a state of serious disequilibrium.

With the major countries being convinced that a world-wide shortage of liquidity is not proven, the efforts of individual nations to pursue an expansionary capital exporting policy can become self-defeating. The net result in the circumstances is that practically all countries end up by operating to a varying extent below capacity, even though reserve levels may not necessarily change much. 'Each of the countries may hesitate to expand production because of a potentially adverse effect on its reserves. . . . In this case the disequilibrium may not only be partial but also universal. This means, in effect, that even if the international exchange markets are in balance, and changes in international liquidity are minimized, the world economy can be out of equilibrium.'[20] The desirable level of reserves for economic purposes cannot therefore be demonstrated objectively, even though needs for international banking purposes can perhaps be so determined. The great danger is that these subjective requirements may be overlooked, leaving a seemingly satisfactory level which in fact is quite unsatisfactory for meeting world economic needs.

[20] Walther Lederer, *The Balance on Foreign Transactions: Problems of Definition and Measurement,* Special Papers in International Finance, Princeton University, No. 5, September 1963, p. 16.

CHAPTER VI

INTERNATIONAL LIQUIDITY FOR ECONOMIC DEVELOPMENT

The tremendous technological break-through over the last half-century has been matched by great changes in both the theory and practice of economics. No longer is poverty assumed to be the inevitable condition for the bulk of mankind. As new nations have arisen from the remnants of mercantile colonialism, each has put forward a claim for a share in the rising world output. Their drive to industrialization has become more than just a matter of welfare, for both political and economic stability could depend upon the poorer countries achieving rates of *per capita* growth approximating those of the richer nations. Otherwise the gap between the high living standards of the industrial countries and the poverty of those who would like to industrialize widens progressively. A closing of the gap in living standards depends upon a vast movement of resources and technical knowledge into under-developed areas, but in a world of imperfect monetary (and political) arrangements, such a capital transfer may well produce enough problems of its own to frustrate many of the attempts.

As mentioned in previous chapters, the transfer of capital in the nineteenth century tended to make the gold standard system work. This co-ordination was due not so much to any virtues of the gold standard but to the particular nature of capital movements over about a century prior to the first world war. During this period capital exports were devoted primarily to the exploitation of natural resources. Raw materials were needed for the growing industrialization of Europe, and particularly of the United Kingdom. With isolated exceptions, this meant the highly populated and underdeveloped countries of today were excluded from these mercantile capital flows. According to Myrdal, 'much the greater part of the capital export from Europe during this era was directed towards those sparsely populated regions in the temperate zones with large natural resources.'[1] Capital movements, in other words, were not directly aimed at raising economic welfare but were geared to the commercial expansion of a complementary international economy based firmly on free trade.

If the gold standard was a casualty of the first world war, it shares its grave with free trade, another victim of those years. Both were necessary to each other and were largely appropriate to the socio-economic system of that period. The gold standard could work because money flows were stabilized; capital movements outwards were normally balanced through repayments with supplies of raw materials. Borrowers and lenders were in harmony and capital investment in transport particularly (at least two-thirds of British foreign investment in the forty years to 1914 being in railways) opened up the granaries of the new world.[2] The complementary nature of the nineteenth century international economy nevertheless worked against the interests of many poorer nations. Free trade plus improved transport ensured that competition from the newly industrialized nations—such as in textiles from Britain—could undercut and dismantle the handicraft competition from poorer countries. 'Indeed,' writes Balogh, 'the opening up of the Indian inland market by railways, far from spreading prosperity, spread ruin.'[3]

Although much has changed since 1914, the need for international capital flows remains unimpaired. In fact, because the world is in the process of disgorging all manner of political and economic changes, including a mitigation of some of the more rapacious elements of mercantile trade, the demand for inter-

[1] Gunner Myrdal, *An International Economy*, New York, Harper, 1956, p. 98.

[2] A. K. Cairncross: "The Contribution of Foreign and Indigenous Capital to Economic Development", *Proceedings of the International Conference of Agricultural Economists*, Eleventh Conference, London, Oxford University Press, 1963, p. 160.

[3] *Unequal Partners, op. cit.*, Vol. 1, p. 11. (Some nineteenth century extractive investment—for example, in Malayan rubber plantations—has also in more recent times facilitated economic development by easing balance of payments pressures.)

national capital is nowadays much greater than ever before. Not only has the indispensability of capital therefore become more apparent, but being less complementary to trade, it also tends nowadays to have a more disruptive effect upon international equilibrium. Of the four main types of capital movements appropriate to the contemporary world, no less than three are inclined to upset equilibrium in the balance of payments sense. The odd man out is the traditional form, for mercantile capital movements still exist: investment and trade in crude oil stand out as the last great example of the nineteenth century model—where investment in a foreign land yielded essential imports for the capital exporting country. The other three forms of capital are different, for generally speaking they seek a return in terms of a command over resources (money) rather than in materials directly. They are, first, short-term capital movements, attracted towards the liquid money market in a foreign land; secondly, long-term private capital in the form that seeks an investment to supply the domestic market in the capital importing country; and long-term governmental capital which seeks primarily to improve human welfare in foreign lands.

Of the three forms of long-term capital, neither private nor governmental transfers have much similarity with the mercantile flows so important in the nineteenth century and earlier.[4] Nowadays, a large proportion of all international private capital investments and most governmental economic aid is related specifically to creating facilities within borrowing countries for supplying the local market rather than foreign markets. In fact, for private capital investment, there are normally franchise restrictions to prevent subsidiaries entering into international competition with the parent company. As subsidiaries frequently comprise the largest and most efficient part of the manufacturing sector in capital importing countries, this means that the recipients may have great difficulties in selling manufactured exports on international markets.

In other words, an importation of capital does not necessarily add to foreign exchange earnings even though the servicing of

[4] A consideration of short-term capital is reserved for Chapter VII because of its special relationship with the international monetary system.

the debt may sooner or later consume foreign exchange in excess of the inflow plus expenditure on imports subsequently saved as a result of the investment. For deficit countries any longer-term balance of payments problems may be masked so long as the capital inflow exceeds debt servicing payments outwards. But borrowing countries could experience great balance of payments problems if the flow of private capital should taper off and especially if a large proportion of all export earnings is consumed in paying remittances abroad. This is one reason why continuing capital movements are so important, for unless the remittances paid to creditor countries are more than balanced by some form of capital outflow from them, the situation could well be one of constant deficit problems in borrowing regions while the creditor countries run chronic balance of payments surpluses. The changed nature of capital movements since the nineteenth century as a result puts much pressure on the international monetary system. Relatively speaking, creditor countries nowadays need much greater reserve levels to ensure that any of their own temporary balance of payments problems do not interrupt the flow of capital that is so necessary for international equilibrium.

Yet the greater proportion of private capital moves between the relatively rich countries, and the problems inherent in a cessation of the flow are usually most painfully apparent in countries like Australia and Canada. It is not easy to envisage how private capital movements can assist in the early stages of the drive to industrialization in the poorer nations. Much of the need of underdeveloped countries is for social overhead capital, in the provision of education and health facilities. Such basic requirements, although needed for ensuring growth, are normally outside the sphere of private enterprise. A United Nations publication shows that the average flow of private long-term capital to thirty-one underdeveloped countries in the 1950's approximated $800 million per annum. Out of these thirty-one countries six of the poorest had an income of less than $100 per head, but from this group—which includes such countries as India and Indonesia—there was actually a net outflow of private capital during the decade.[5]

[5] United Nations, *World Economic Survey 1960*, p. 65.

SECOND THOUGHTS ABOUT ECONOMIC AID

In the 1950's the inadequacy of private capital flows was partly offset when the richer industrial countries—and particularly the United States—began to devote governmental capital in substantial amounts towards the economic development of the poorer countries. With the help of advances in economic theory, attitudes had shifted away from viewing poverty as being fundamentally inevitable and the aim was now extended beyond just containing communism. The example of the Marshall Aid rehabilitation of a prostrate Europe demonstrated how massive capital transfers could speedily and successfully prime the pump for economic growth. But by the early 1960's much of the idealism of the previous decade had worn a little thin. For one thing, the recipients of economic aid did not always choose democratic capitalism as a way of life, and in some more unstable areas simply used economic assistance as a cushion to cover reality rather than as a ladder to higher living standards. Then secondly, the quick results that had been demonstrated by Marshall Aid seemed to be singularly lacking in many underdeveloped countries, and with balance of payments problems of its own, the United States faced growing difficulties in maintaining a continuously increasing flow of capital overseas for developmental purposes.

With such a disappointing record by comparison with initial hopes, second thoughts about economic aid have been most forcefully expressed in the United States, the country which has made by far the highest contribution. Comparisons have been drawn between the success of Marshall Aid on the one hand and the relative failure of aid to underdeveloped countries on the other, with the aim of showing the unrewarding nature of the more recent assistance. But such an identification is scarcely fair or realistic. Economic aid despatched to Europe early in the post-war years was directed towards a collapsed community which was nevertheless literate and well developed in its commercial and technical attributes. All these are important characteristics, basic to sustained growth, and sadly lacking in most underdeveloped nations. Marshall Aid in effect supplied Europe both quickly and easily with the means of acquiring a new stock of capital for an area well endowed with natural and human resources. With economic aid acting as a primer in such a favourable environment, Europe was soon able to reach a position where growth not only became self-supporting, but where living standards expanded each year at compounded rates. In a matter of years, pre-war living standards were left far behind.

The background in the underdeveloped countries is remarkably different. Not only is there a considerable shortage of capital; not only is the ready availability of raw materials usually restricted; but the basic skills and social climate in which to utilize twentieth century techniques are also normally absent. Compared with Marshall Aid to Europe, economic assistance to underdeveloped countries represents a much greater challenge. The ground to be covered is more extensive as much of it is concerned with the provision of social overhead capital—itself normally a prerequisite to self-sustained growth.

In fact the dawning and growing awareness of the magnitude of the task seems to influence politicians and administrators in a variety of ways. First, there is that small but vocal group for whom the problem has become so difficult as to be insoluble. In their view all aid should be discontinued. Then there is a much more powerful middle group which feels the richer countries of Western Europe should share much more equitably the burden of giving and that the recipients should be those countries following the concepts of capitalism and democracy. The flow of aid capital is assumed to be a fairly temporary phenomenon, tapering off as the investment leads in a few years to rising living standards. To this group the basic reason for giving aid and judging its effectiveness concerns its ability to obstruct communism. Aid for purely economic reasons may call in discussion about the burden of assistance. This does not mean that the protagonists of this attitude would not continue aid if the cold war ended, but it does mean that with a cold war in progress, the economic priorities and absolute quantities of aid are frequently given second position to military considerations. The views of this middle group, currently quite strong in the United States, are a

89

reasonable expression of the opinion embodied in the influential Clay Report.[6]

There is another group whose views are frequently to be found in academic circles and in the United Nations, and who are rather dismayed at the political overtones of much aid-giving. They recognize the impracticability of expecting quick results, especially as *per capita* advances are usually held back by population growth. But, most important, it is understood that if aid to under-developed countries is to be effective, the total must be increased, not reduced. In other words, this group realizes the important differences between aid to an exhausted Europe and aid to the emergent nations.

Nevertheless it is sometimes possible to stimulate economic development in poorer countries without any outside economic assistance, private or governmental Russian economic growth in the early five-year planning periods after 1928 is a good example. The basis for this approach is found in a totalitarian political state willing and able to force the mass of the population to accept—or even reduce—its present living standards. Then in place of any early increase in national income contributing to a forward movement in living standards, the marginal advance is instead saved for new capital investment. From the planner's point of view, therefore, totalitarian systems have one particular advantage: overriding authority can be used to ensure that increases in output are invested rather than consumed, no matter how poor the population.

In democratic countries one of the major problems of economic development lies in the method of pushing output ahead of any growth in consumption—for if an increasing proportion of the national income does not go towards investment, it is difficult to raise productivity and *per capita* incomes. Without discussing the technical and humanitarian problems associated with achieving such a goal, the facts of the situation suggest that savings are falling in underdeveloped countries. According to one official report, 'a rather paradoxical development in the nineteen-fifties has been that, while ever-increasing importance has been

[6] United States. Department of State, *The Scope and Distribution of United States Military and Economic Assistance Programs*, Washington, March 1963.

attached to the aim of accelerating economic growth, domestic saving in relation to gross national product has risen in no more than one-third of the underdeveloped countries. . . . In about half the countries, in fact, levels of domestic saving have declined."[7] This trend suggests that in democratic societies there is a limit to the additional amounts of finance obtainable from internal sources when people are trying to achieve and want to obtain some tiny immediate increase in living standards.

Although it is sometimes suggested that the richer income groups in underdeveloped countries could supply more development finance through taxation, the simple demographic fact (without considering any tax collection problems) is that the rich are proportionately so few that their share of the national income is much less than in Western countries. Nevertheless this does not mean that domestic saving in underdeveloped countries will not remain the most important source of finance for economic development. It is just that squeezing out marginal additions is a formidable task in non-totalitarian countries.

A third method of financing developmental programmes is for developing countries to draw down their reserves of international liquidity. In the past, several underdeveloped countries have used this technique, especially during the earlier post-war years when blocked sterling balances were gradually released. The situation has changed since the Korean War, for the terms of trade have moved against most of the underdeveloped regions in a period when many developmental plans—and the associated pressure on reserves—were first introduced. The collective reserves of the thirteen Afro-Asian countries, for example, fell 32 per cent between 1953 and 1963.[8]

Although richer countries can more readily afford to hold reserves than their poorer neighbours, it is the poorer primary producing countries which in many respects have the greater need.[9] The price of primary products is notoriously unstable, even if the products concerned do not suffer the further hazard of being

[7] United Nations, *op. cit.*, p. 85.

[8] Burma, Ceylon, Ghana, India, Malaya, Pakistan, Taiwan, Congo, United Arab Republic, Ethiopia, Indonesia, Philippines and Thailand.

[9] See Thomas Balogh, "International Reserves and Liquidity", *The Economic Journal*, June 1960, p. 364.

replaced by synthetic alternatives. In addition, most of the poorer countries are dependent upon the export of a single commodity. In fact no less than eighteen underdeveloped countries rely upon one product for one-half or more of their export income—the product being either sugar, coffee, cocoa, rubber or tin, and each of these is well known for being erratic and uncertain in price behaviour.[10] Unless international reserves, extra foreign aid or compensatory finance from the International Monetary Fund can take up all the slack in changing export income, developmental plans are therefore too frequently tied to changing harvests and export prices.[11] Reserves, as the name suggests, are normally better used as "buffers" against an uncertain future and for giving continuity to development than as capital for developmental purposes.

An underdeveloped country can build up its reserves while paying for developmental imports if it sells more abroad. In poorer countries, in fact, the ability to earn foreign exchange is even more important for ensuring steady economic growth than in the richer countries. In contrast to developed countries, economic expansion in emergent nations has a particularly strong effect upon the demand for foreign exchange, for the developmental process itself gives what Reddaway has called a structural shift in the propensity to import.[12] Simply because the country itself is underdeveloped, equipment and technical facilities cannot be very readily supplied from internal sources, so much of the capital equipment needed must be imported.

The pressure on imports arising from economic development is particularly noticeable in countries where international trade is quantitatively small compared with national income. In these circumstances, and although the imports for development may be only a small part of national income, they can nevertheless represent a large part of export earnings. The magnitude of this frequently overlooked element can be thrown into relief by comparing Australia, a country with a large amount of trade rela-

[10] "Commodities and the Underdeveloped Countries", *Westminster Bank Review*, August 1963, p. 28.

[11] See Ian Shannon, *Australian Trade with Asia*, Committee of Economic Development of Australia, 1962, p. 18.

[12] W. B. Reddaway, "The Economics of Under-Developed Countries", *The Economic Journal*, March 1963, p. 7.

tive to national income, with the quite different situation of India. In Australia capital imports equal to one per cent of national income are equivalent to about 5 per cent of export earnings. In India, by contrast, capital imports equal to one per cent of national income approximate 22 per cent of Indian earnings of foreign exchange. Expressed differently it is possible to say that importing equipment into Australia up to the level of 5 per cent of national income over a given period only takes about one-quarter of all foreign exchange earnings; in India an equivalent importation exceeds the total of the country's export earnings.

Indeed, from the point of view of achieving satisfactory economic growth in developing countries, the importance of expanding the frontiers of trade (or aid) extends even further. If trade can expand quickly, underdeveloped countries are also able to minimize any harmful side-effects of planning and entrepreneurial errors, thus hastening the time when they reach take-off and growth at compound rates of increase. In the course of development—even in rich countries, let alone poor ones—it is difficult to avoid over-capacity in some sectors and under-capacity in others at particular times. In underdeveloped countries the scope for importing goods to make up for temporary short-falls or excesses in production is limited. These characteristics of development can produce admixtures of surpluses and bottlenecks. But on the reasonable assumption that an expanding proportion of trade to national income allows a broadening of the local market from national boundaries towards the whole international trading area, an increased flow of both exports and imports greatly facilitates a more even meshing of supply and demand. Expanding the frontiers of trade therefore reduces and can even offset the economic costs of investment mistakes.

These characteristics make an expansion of exports from underdeveloped countries the most important single factor influencing their economic growth. Whatever the amount of aid, trade must finance the greater proportion of import requirements for economic development. From 1956 to 1959, for example, one report shows that exports provided the underdeveloped countries with six times more exchange than they obtained from total net long-term inflows and official donations.[13] The narrative, in fact, comes back to the terms of trade and the associated possibility of the richer industrial countries taking more imports from the emergent nations. According to Nurkse, the primary exporting countries earned an extra three to four billion dollars in 1951 because of the favourable terms of trade in that year.[14] The United Nations *World Economic Report* for 1958 estimated that the worsening of the terms of trade between 1957 and 1958 cut the income of poor countries by far more than the total aid they received.[15] The figures imply that the richer nations must consider whether they can accommodate more exports from underdeveloped countries. But in ensuring their own growth the richer countries have tended to make adjustments through restricting imports from underdeveloped countries. In this regard the Secretary-General of the United Nations, U Thant, made a telling point when he wrote: '. . . precisely because they are so advanced, the high-income countries should be able to alleviate any hardships without shifting the burden of adjustment to the developing countries by restricting the latter's export markets.'[16]

Without doubting the importance of international trade as the principal springboard to self-sustained economic growth, it is difficult to be sanguine about the future potential from the point of view of the underdeveloped countries. As shown on pages 79-81, the gap between the import needs and export receipts of the poorer countries is likely to widen while they remain underdeveloped, for technological change has rendered many of their traditional exports absolutely or relatively obsolete. Their import requirements are certainly clear enough. The United Nations estimates that if the import capacity of underdeveloped countries (as based on export earnings) is not to deteriorate further, then by 1970 the exports of all the underdeveloped countries will have to reach approximately $45 billion per annum (and this is with-

[13] United Nations, Department of Economic and Social Affairs, *The United Nations Development Decade, Proposals for Action*, New York, 1962, p. 75.

[14] Ragnar Nurkse: *Problems of Capital Formation in Underdeveloped Countries*, Oxford, Basil Blackwell, 1953, p. 97.

[15] Quoted by Balogh, *Unequal Partners, op. cit.*, Vol. 2, p. 37.

[16] *The United Nations Development Decade, op. cit.*, p. vii.

out making allowance for debt repayment commitments).[17] Yet in 1962 exports from underdeveloped countries were only about $28 billion, and the need for rapid annual increases is therefore apparent. Such a herculean task is thrown into relief when it is noted that in 1953 their exports were $20·4 billion, for on a rate of increase equal to that of the last decade, total exports would rise to only about $35 to $38 billion by 1970. The short-fall on trade alone could be about $10 billion a year. Debt remittances will nevertheless have also increased, thereby inflating requirements beyond this amount. The International Development Association estimates that the total debt of the underdeveloped countries doubled to $20 billion over the five years ended 1961, and forecasts the figure will reach at least $30 billion by 1967.[18]

Another study, quite different in scope and nature, supports the contention that the underdeveloped countries will face growing problems in finding adequate foreign exchange to pay for the imports needed. According to Maizels, the capital inflow requirements of all the primary exporting countries collectively will increase from the level of some $7 billion a year in the late 1950's to between about $13 billion and $18 billion by 1970-75. The crucial importance of aid for economic development is thus emphasized. Even if export earnings grow at the maximum likely rate, there is no other way: economic aid represents the residual means of ensuring that economic development moves ahead of population growth in less developed countries.

SECOND THOUGHTS ABOUT THE LEVEL OF LIQUIDITY

The very idea of economic aid for development is coming under increasing criticism even though such assistance, if made available sensibly and on a sufficient scale, represents the only way the mass of the world's people can escape poverty. To improve the quality of aid so that the critics may be quietened means that programmes must be built into the social environment

[17] *ibid.*, p. 75.
[18] Quoted in *Business Week*, New York, 7 December 1963, p. 110.

of recipient countries, not just placed on top. As noted earlier, there is a great deal of difference between making aid available to devastated but technically advanced countries—such as Europe in the early post-war period—and underdeveloped countries.

The concept of aid for economic development should go further than the idea of giving capital in the form of physical goods. In underdeveloped countries there is a need for changed social and technical attitudes as a prerequisite to sustained growth, and for this reason much of the initial work must literally be accomplished in the field among the great mass of population. Seemingly simple things are sometimes the most important: teaching farmers the advantages of using fertilizer and improved seeds and how to raise egg production are perfect examples of this unspectacular but urgently needed form of assistance. One United Nations report illustrates in eloquent terms the need for technical aid. 'To offset the population pressure,' the report indicates, 'one of the obvious means of increasing income and capital formation is to make the fullest possible use of the human resources—the abundant factor. This can be done both quantitatively and qualitatively—quantitatively by increasing employment and reducing under-employment, qualitatively by improving the health, education and technical training of the people and reducing disguised unemployment so as to raise productivity. . . . Although it is a controversial question how much surplus labour can be absorbed into productive activities with reasonable returns if not backed by considerable natural resources and capital, the problem is being attacked to some extent. . . . On a much smaller scale, several other countries also are increasing their efforts to make use of their surplus labour for capital formation or in other productive ways, through community developmental projects or similar schemes. These activities include the construction of roads, houses and canals, the digging of irrigation wells, more intensive cultivation, the development of household handicrafts, etc.'[19] Yet, given the need, the total technical assistance expenditure in 1961 was only $470 million—under 8 per cent of the total bilateral aid figure of $6·1 billion.[20]

[19] United Nations, *Economic Bulletin for Asia and the Far East*, Vol. X, No. 1, June 1959, p. 45.
[20] United Nations, *World Economic Survey for 1962*, pp. 111 and 118.

If, instead of looking at the quality of aid, attention is directed towards its geographic spread, then much of the assistance would seem to be misplaced. The Clay Report indicates that no less than 72 per cent of the total United States military and economic appropriations have gone to those countries bordering on communist territory.[21] A country's position on the globe thus largely determines its appropriation. While there are probably sound reasons for such a state of affairs, it does suggest that aid for economic growth may frequently bypass those countries which can use it most effectively, and gives a different interpretation to the view that existing levels of assistance are beyond the collective absorption ability of the poorer countries. A United Nations report highlights this point when, for example, it is shown that over the decade of the fifties no less than 38 per cent of the net cumulative long-term capital and official donations to Asian countries went to two countries, the Republic of Korea and the Republic of Vietnam, although their proportion of the population was only 4 per cent.[22] Another study gives further emphasis to the extraordinary disparity between recipient countries in terms of funds actually made available. For instance, over the three years ended 1959, the average annual aid varied from 41 cents per head of population in Egypt to over $36 per head in Jordan.[23] *Per capita* aid to different underdeveloped countries is expressive both of political and population considerations. But to raise aid in India from current levels of around 75 cents *per capita* each year to the figure for Chile of just on $8 (which itself is less than one-quarter of the amount going to Jordan) would entail a further outlay to India *alone* of $2·9 billion each year. But over the five years to 1960 India received an average of only $375 million net each year from official and banking sources.[24]

Continuing with India as the example, it is possible to approach the problem another way. Over the ten years ended

[21] *op. cit.*, p. 5.
[22] United Nations, *Economic Bulletin for Asia and the Far East*, Vol. XIII, No. 3, December 1962, Table 3, p. 54.
[23] United Nations, *International Economic Assistance to the Less Developed Countries*, New York, 1961, Table 27, p. 45.
[24] United Nations, *Economic Bulletin for Asia and the Far East, op. cit.*, Table 4, p. 56.

1959, net domestic saving was equal to 7 per cent of gross national product, while the equivalent aid and grants received were equal to a further 0·3 per cent.[25] If capital inflow from abroad was to raise investment levels to 14 per cent of gross national product—as it is in Burma—then the annual transfer would need to increase by $1·8 billion. If investment in India increased to 20 per cent of gross national product (which represents the situation in many richer countries), then the additional annual capital inflow would need to be at least $3·4 billion. Therefore the example of one country alone, whether based on a consideration of *per capita* requirements or in terms of investment needs, shows the magnitude of the challenge. India alone would absorb at least $3 billion each year.

The general line of argument suggests two propositions, interconnected perhaps but nevertheless different in nature. One is that aid should be more appropriate—appropriate not only in form but to the stage of economic development. The other concerns the need for a much increased level of economic assistance by Western donor countries currently in a mood to cut aid from present-day total levels of around $9 billion per annum, and despite the fact that income in the affluent part of the world increases each year by much more than this amount.[26]

How, then, can the effectiveness of aid be improved? The need for more suitable aid has been noted—aid capable of inducing a change in attitudes within poorer countries well away from the traditionalism appropriate to thinking in pre-industrial Europe. But from the point of view of the donor countries this can produce balance of payments difficulties, for

[25] United Nations, *World Economic Survey for 1960*, pp. 62-4, although, as pointed out in another publication, there has in more recent years been a gratifying increase where the net flow of assistance reached 1·3 per cent of Indian gross national product and 6·9 per cent of gross domestic investment over the five years to 1960 (*Economic Bulletin for Asia and the Far East*, December 1962, p. 64).

[26] Although there may be little merit in many comparisons, it is of some interest in the present context to look at estimates produced by the University of Michigan's Survey Research Centre. Citizens of the United States currently give domestically about $17 billion to churches and charity each year, and on this basis the average American family redistributes approximately $300 or 5 per cent of personal income after payment of taxes. About $6 billion of the total goes to churches and over $7 billion to needy United States citizens. (Quoted in *The Economist*, 24 February 1962, p. 710.)

the assistance must then be spent largely within recipient countries. Completely tied aid exported in the form of food or capital equipment (and assuming for simplicity that it is as grants rather than loans) need not induce balance of payments problems because such aid given to recipient countries in terms of the donor's currency is in effect swapped back again into physical commodities. But untied aid—and technical assistance within the boundaries of recipient countries particularly—can be largely spent outside the donor's country. There is no guarantee that exports from the donor will rise either immediately or even eventually on a sufficient scale to balance the monetary transfer. In this respect the effect of technical aid upon the balance of payments is similar to military expenditure by service personnel stationed abroad.

Such factors would seem to be at the root of some of the vacillation frequently displayed by donor governments in making decisions about economic aid.[27] Greatly expanded aid must mean a much increased transfer of reserves from individual donor countries, and if the aid is largely in the form of technical assistance within recipient countries, or if it is free from ties as to the direction of its expenditure, then the erosion of reserves is proportionately increased. Nowadays 80 per cent of American aid must be spent on procurement from United States suppliers. But even then it is impossible to stop all leakages of international reserves from donor countries. The Brookings Institution forecasts that the United States in 1968 could still be losing $1·17 billion a year even with very strict control over leakages.[28] A leakage of this dimension, although insignificant against some aggregates like the United States gross national product, represents no less than 8·3 per cent of the total American gold reserves at September 1965. By itself, therefore, such a leakage could consume the entire American gold stock in thirteen years. If the richer countries shared aid commitments more equitably, this leakage from the United States may be reduced somewhat. Even with any equitable basis of sharing, the United States would still be giving over one-half of the total assistance. But

[27] See also, Organisation for Economic Co-operation and Development, *Development Assistance Efforts and Policies*, 1963 Review, p. 36.

[28] *The United States Balance of Payments in 1968, op. cit.*, p. 174.

in periods when the United States is less competitive than most other industrial countries, the returning expenditure may be only a small proportion of total aid outlay.

The desire of officials in donor countries to conserve international reserves through ensuring that as much aid as possible is bilateral and tied to physical goods finds ready support in business circles. More or less by accident, aid policies introduced with the purpose of minimizing drains on international reserves may turn into export stimulation subsidies for manufacturing interests. This intensifying bilateralism could mean lending governments will become associated more and more with their own export industries in an effort to outbid or outsell all rivals. For recipient countries it could mean being lured into more and more costly projects based not on the economic needs of the underdeveloped country itself but instead upon the economic structure of the aid-supplying country.[29] In the circumstances recipient countries (and particularly those propped-up states near communist borders) have difficulty in using the ill-conceived and ill-directed physical goods efficiently. The final irony then comes when the critics suggest aid cuts both in total and for all countries individually.

The uncertainty of aid programmes was neatly summarized in a comment on Asian economic development plans when it was stated that if underdeveloped countries '. . . are required to undertake such projects in an atmosphere of uncertainty regarding the availability of external assistance, such plans are likely to be undertaken and executed in a haphazard fashion, thereby jeopardising the whole fabric of economic development. As a matter of fact, development programmes must be thought of in terms of decades not years and, in order to encourage . . . countries to undertake such long-range and effective planning, they must be provided with a reasonable assurance of continued external assistance at least for the whole plan period.'[30] The world must accept the challenge. An expansion of suitably based economic aid can enlarge gross national product throughout the world. A restriction of aid below the optimum, on the other

---

[29] See Charles J. V. Murphy, "Foreign Aid: Billions in Search of a Good Reason", *Fortune*, March 1963, *passim*.

[30] *Economic Bulletin for Asia and the Far East*, December 1962, p. 67.

hand, and tailored to fit current liquidity levels and its distribution, can hinder the expansion of latent international trade in addition to impeding development within poorer countries.

The present-day aid programmes may also increase the balance of payments difficulties of the underdeveloped countries. As noted earlier, there is always a problem of servicing capital when its aim is to increase domestic production rather than export production. But with badly oriented capital flows there is little possibility even in the long run that indirect benefits will yield import replacing or export stimulating characteristics sufficient to cover the repayments including interest. Naturally, with very low rates of interest or loans free of interest, the need to invest in projects with good immediate returns is less pressing. But in 1961, for example, no less than 72 per cent of all bilateral loan commitments to underdeveloped countries carried interest rates in excess of 5 per cent and 30 per cent of all such transfers had to be repaid in less than ten years.[31] Over recent years the debt service payments have increased, and even in 1960-61 the burden of repayments represented over 13 per cent of all merchandise exports for the underdeveloped countries.[32] According to the International Development Association, debt servicing costs have been growing alarmingly. By 1966, in India, for example, service on the present debt alone will take 26 per cent of all export earnings, and new obligations will have to be added.[33]

Clearly the position is both unsatisfactory and unstable, but without an overall increase in the total of world reserves the hands of the donors are largely tied. If governmental aid is more generous in terms and more suited in form from the point of view of the underdeveloped country, it may take many years —if not decades—for an outward flow of capital to be reflected as a net surplus in the balance of payments of the country making the original transfer. On the other hand, a drying up of the flow of capital—as shown by the experience of the late twenties and the thirties—can be particularly difficult for deficit countries. Instead of the continuing capital inflow covering the debt servicing costs on past external borrowing, all such charges

---

[31] *World Economic Survey for 1962, op. cit.*, p. 116.
[32] *ibid.*, p. 114.
[33] *Business Week, ibid.*

payable in foreign currencies then have to be met out of current export earnings.

The present-day world is in a dilemma. In the poorer countries an increase in external assistance is needed for both balance of payments reasons and welfare considerations. But increased allocations from the richer countries could produce such a drain on the reserves of individual donors that corrective action becomes imperative. Yet it is important that no major creditor country should be forced either to cut down or call in long-term lending to meet short-term balance of payments commitments, or to seek to borrow short-term to maintain long-term lending. Both policies can produce instability—the former through causing stagnation to world trade and payments, and the latter through endangering the gold exchange standard.

Fundamentally the choice facing the world boils down to the alternatives of increasing the total level of international liquidity to match the long-term capital-outflow/repayment-inflow cycle more closely, or to limit the capital transfers below the optimum for achieving balance in the international economy. If a decision is made in favour of the first alternative (in other words, if it is agreed that the international monetary system shall serve world economic needs and not the other way round), then the urgent requirement is to create more *net* reserves without a credit nexus. An increase in *gross* reserves—through, for example, an expansion of borrowing facilities—only begs the question, for each addition to the total quantity of reserves presupposes a proportional shortening of the uncommitted net reserves outstanding.

Some indication of the size of the increase required is apparent from the figures showing the needs of the world economy. For reasons outlined above and in Chapter V, it is apparent that the future external capital requirements of the underdeveloped countries will be between $15 and $20 billion each year if the servicing cost of previous debts is not to produce such balance of payments crisis as to force at least some debtor countries into default—or introduce other complications if a moratorium becomes inevitable. If the nature of future aid and its conditions are reasonably favourable, then there will be less pressure on the balance of payments of underdeveloped countries and the lower limit of about $15 billion could cover the capital inflow necessary for secure economic development.

$15 billion is equal to 1·4 per cent of the 1964 gross national product of the ten major donor countries collectively, and 2·5 per cent of that of the United States—America being richer than all the other nine countries put together.[34] Such a transfer in itself should not represent any particular strain on the resources of the donor countries; after all, in 1944, the United States defence outlays were over 40 per cent of the American gross national product at the time.[35] But if the governments of the richer countries should be willing to commit themselves to the welfare of the majority of mankind, the transfer problem with limited reserves remains. It is important to remember that although $15 billion approximates but 1·4 per cent of the gross national product of the major donor countries (and is therefore less than the average annual increase in income), it is also equivalent to just over one-half of the June 1964 gold reserves (that is *net* or "owned" reserves) of the same ten countries.

The present-day position is untenable. Even with tied aid there can be a considerable leakage to other markets, either more competitive or satisfactory in some other way. Temporary losses of reserves to the particular industrial country temporarily most competitive would not cause so much balance of payments concern to other donors if they had a greater reserve cover. If the existing net reserves of the ten donor countries were tripled, then instead of an annual appropriation of $15 billion representing one-half of their collective reserves, it would be reduced to less than one-fifth. Such an increase in reserves—although not so high as to erase caution—could nevertheless give donors sufficient liquidity to maintain the required international capital flows without too much regard for immediate reserve losses and total reserve holdings *vis-à-vis* other countries. In these circumstances not only would the international monetary system be

[34] The countries being Australia, Belgium, Canada, France, West Germany, Japan, Netherlands, Sweden, United Kingdom and the United States.
[35] United States. Congress, Joint Economic Committee, Study Paper No. 18, *National Security and the American Economy in the 1960's*, by Henry Rowen, p. 68.

lubricating the world economy, but the process itself, and especially if an increase in liquidity could be coupled with some continuing commitment as to economic aid, represents the single opportunity of most people for obtaining economic salvation.

CHAPTER VII

INTERNATIONAL LIQUIDITY FOR MONETARY STABILITY

The gold exchange standard is something of a hybrid. Its reserves comprise two forms of money having a quite different origin. The size of one depends mainly upon the success of mining and Soviet gold sales to the West, while the size of the other depends upon the fortuitous circumstances of how far the balance of payments of the key currency countries are—or have been—in surplus (or deficit). The use of gold as international reserves seems at first glance even more quaint than employing dollars or sterling. Gold is no longer used as a national currency in any country, whereas dollars and sterling are in everyday use within the borders of two important trading nations as well as internationally.

Yet the problems associated with the gold exchange standard do not arise from the employment of gold as international money but from the use of national money for this purpose. Nor is it difficult to find the reason for this seeming inconsistency. Gold is still accepted as the ultimate or final store of value, and the strength of national currencies when used internationally depends largely upon their gold backing. There are a variety of philosophic and commercial reasons based on history and tradition which determine the order of monetary importance or precedence between metallic money and paper money, and it seems unlikely that the sequence will change at all quickly in the future. Indeed, in a world of rapid economic change and many political uncertainties, the basic standing of gold becomes, if anything, more secure. Gold is no longer used nationally simply because its monetary importance transcends a localized role.

H

Recent history has demonstrated some of the problems of using national money as international obligations. Just as gold in the form of a liquid reserve takes precedence over all national currencies, different national currencies themselves rank in order. At any time the national money most generally acceptable as a key currency is likely to be the scarcest or "hardest" currency—which invariably means the money of a large and powerful trading and banking country with the strongest tendency to run a sizable surplus in its balance of payments. There will be a flow of gold towards this country from those in deficit to it, and since it will naturally also accept its own currency in place of gold, the currency concerned is "as good as gold". But while the country is in surplus and its money is both hard and as good as gold, the self-same money will also be extremely scarce internationally, thereby doing little to add to the total of world liquidity.[1]

It is only by running into deficit that the key currency country can add significantly to the total of world liquidity. But in doing so a point of saturation can eventually be reached where the country's liquid debts to foreigners become so large compared with its own stock of gold that the key currency becomes progressively less hard and not such a perfect substitute for gold. Every increase in the total foreign exchange outstanding reduces the gold cover ratio, bringing with it a continuous decline in the willingness of other countries to hold the national currency of the key currency country as international reserves.

A SYSTEM IN DESPAIR

Because the gold exchange standard has these characteristics, its operation is less than perfect. In fact the troubles with the mechanism as a working system can be conveniently listed under three headings, each of which can be distinctly embarrassing, as policy decisions about any of them can be caught on the horns of a dilemma. First, there is the dilemma attendant upon creating sufficient international reserves to meet the longer-term needs

[1] See Robert Collin, "What's Going on Now in World Finance", *The Director*, August 1963, p. 264.

of a dynamic international economy; then there is the exchange rate dilemma which can arise when national money is used internationally; and, thirdly, there is the dilemma of national interest rates involved in the switching of funds between countries as investors seek the best international return. Each of these dilemmas is conceptually independent from the others and may well be dormant at any particular time. But if one should be causing trouble it can have the effect of making the other dilemmas arise in concert.

The liquidity dilemma is basic to the mechanism of the gold exchange standard—and is in fact nowadays the source of several difficulties. When a key currency country experiences a deficit in the balance of payments there is an increase in gross world reserves but not necessarily in net world reserves. Although the exchange component represents an increase in the liquidity of the holding country, it should largely be regarded as a diminution of liquidity in the issuing country by the amount of the liability. Fundamentally an increase in reserves under the gold exchange standard depends upon newly mined gold and Soviet sales. If a key currency country remains in deficit to the extent of causing holders of its currency to seek a transfer to gold, the entire system may collapse. Thus although the key currency system implies a rationing of scarce gold, it nevertheless has great difficulty in achieving this aim. The United States, in seeking to solve one side of the problem by pursuing policies that bring her external accounts into surplus—and thus harden the dollar—also endangers the international economy to the extent that gross world reserves will fall as dollars held abroad are repatriated to pay the excess of foreign debits over credits with America. Thus as matters stand there is no possibility of doing the "right" thing: appropriate action in one direction leads to harmful consequences in the other. Solving the deficit could reintroduce the dollar shortage; leaving the deficit unsolved increases at each step the difficulty of encouraging foreigners to hold dollars instead of gold.

The exchange rate dilemma—the second fundamental problem of the gold exchange standard—is most directly concerned with the key currency countries. The gold exchange standard does not itself produce any instability in the rate of exchange of the key

107

currency countries (or doubts about the future rate), provided the quantity of exchange held in foreign hands is relatively small. In other words, when the gold exchange standard is not working in such a way as to create new reserves, there may be little pressure on the exchange rate. But when the quantity of exchange held abroad is high compared with the gold backing in the key currency countries—that is, when the gold exchange standard is meeting the objective of economizing in the use of gold—there may well be considerable anxiety about the future rate of exchange. With little key currency being held as reserves by other countries, the exchange rate of the key currency countries could be sound, but then there may well be insufficient international liquidity for world requirements. With sound exchange rates and confidence there may be a willingness to build up the key currency component—which in turn gives rise to second thoughts about holding exchange as international reserves.

With the gold exchange standard one problem leads to another, for uncertainties about the future rate of exchange can occur when the liquidity dilemma is also apparent. In fact the liquidity dilemma itself is pressing at such times because of the uncertainties about the future rate of exchange. But from the point of view of the key currency countries, the exchange rate dilemma tends to exist at all times, for neither a unilateral devaluation nor a unilateral appreciation is at all easy, even if the political difficulties of a change in par are overcome.[2] A unilateral devaluation inflicts a loss in terms of gold for those countries holding the devaluating currency as reserves and, to judge by the experience of the inter-war years, can throw up monetary chaos in its wake. A gold guarantee on dollar or sterling liabilities would avoid this difficulty, but would instead reduce what is in fact a strong incentive to devalue such currencies—the fact that it reduces the value of the devaluing country's liquid liabilities compared with its liquid assets. A unilateral appreciation in a key currency country has the opposite effect. The gold value of the national currency then rises in proportion to the appreciation, and this means not only that the gold cover to its key currency liabilities diminishes accordingly, but

2 See pages 62-3.

also that the value of world reserves in terms of the key currency concerned is reduced.[3] In the circumstances, and regardless of the longer-term consequences, the maintenance of the existing rate of exchange has seeming advantages. The international monetary emphasis is therefore on a fixed rate of exchange in perpetuity, even though the achievement of optimum domestic and international equilibrium may depend upon a change.

The third problem posed by the gold exchange standard concerns the dilemma of short-term rates of interest (the bank rate). It occurs because movements in the rate of interest, especially under general convertibility, can cause quick changes in the position of the balance of payments, besides influencing the level of activity within the domestic economy. A comparatively small change in the rate of interest in one country, relative to the rate of interest in other countries, may swing a large volume of lending from one to the other. In contrast, the balance of trade position is by no means so sensitive. This is at the heart of the matter, for it is impossible to change flows of trade quickly to meet short-term money movements. 'This high degree of short-period mobility of international lending,' according to Keynes, 'combined with a low degree of short-term mobility of international trade, means—failing steps to deal with the former—that even a small and temporary divergence in the local rate of interest from the international rate may be dangerous.'[4]

A. E. Jasay outlined the nature of this dilemma in evidence to the Radcliffe Committee when he said, 'cases may occur . . . where the authorities see no valid reason for cutting down home demand, feel no anxiety about the present and future balance of current payments, and regard speculative fears of devaluation

---

[3] Since the United States at present purchases gold from central banks without limit at $35 an ounce, the international price of the metal cannot fall below this amount. If the United States changed this policy by rescinding this obligation, and without counter-proposals as to a new price, it is difficult to forecast gold price trends in relation to the United States dollar. But without a new international currency both generally and automatically acceptable without limit, the only likely alternative to the less secure dollar would be gold, and a transfer of demand to gold on a large scale could produce a considerable depreciation of the dollar. For this reason demonetizing gold may have the perverse effect of raising its price in terms of dollars and other national currencies.

[4] J. M. Keynes, *A Treatise on Money*, Vol. II, *op. cit.*, p. 309.

as unfounded; and yet the strength of those fears, reflected in a flight into foreign currencies, forces them to take defensive action. This is when the bank rate dilemma becomes painfully acute; for bank rate acts indiscriminately on both fronts, hitting the domestic economy even if it was not intended to do so.'[5]

With convertibility (and especially with resident convertibility) other countries besides the key currency countries may be plagued with the interest rate dilemma: it arises when any country faces a shortage of reserves, and this malady can be widespread. Indeed the need for reserves in this context is to avoid the general stagnation which occurs if several important countries engage in a competitive bidding up of interest rates in response to the dilemma. Edward M. Bernstein, for example, has written that the large industrial countries need 'large reserves of their own in order to have greater autonomy in dealing with payments difficulties, when they occur, without imposing severe restrictions on international trade and investment or undue restraints on domestic economic activity.'[6]

Being based on a shortage of reserves, the dilemma with the rate of interest becomes acute in a key currency country when it is in deficit; that is, when it is probably concerned with the other problems associated with the gold exchange standard. The dilemma is represented by a choice between long- or short-term palliatives, for the short-term techniques of preserving intact limited net reserves may at times have the perverse effect of either inducing (or intensifying further) any secular trend towards stagnation and unemployment. Such a situation is particularly applicable to key currency countries when they have to choose between making the best of their domestic economic potential on one side, or strengthening their international monetary position on the other. The normal short-term deflationary bias arising out of the need to strengthen the balance of payments can create a longer-term slackening of economic growth (especially as compared with non-reserve countries) and ensure a steady continuance of succeeding crises and further deflation-

[5] United Kingdom, Committee on the Working of the Monetary System, *Memoranda of Evidence*, Vol. 3, p. 132.
[6] "A Practical Program for International Monetary Reserves", *Quarterly Review*, Model, Roland and Co., New York, Fourth Quarter, 1963, p. 4.

ary periods. In other words, once a key currency country has actually become entangled with this problem, the dilemma of the bank rate has a bias towards perpetuity. Financial crises become more prevalent as each short-term solution further saps the country's remaining economic vigour. The United Kingdom has been caught in this predicament for decades and Balogh gives a graphic description of the symptoms when he writes: 'The years 1927, 1931 and 1937 mark the . . . external pre-war crises. Crisis milestones in the post-war period are 1947, 1949, 1951, 1955, 1957, 1959-61. Ten crises. All are of the same pattern. All, without exception, were responded to by the same old method of restriction, accompanied by a monotonous chorus of ministerial platitudes, echoed in the City, about the need to "stiffen our economy", "cut the cloth", and so on. Meanwhile, first the Soviet Union, then Germany, then Japan (soon it will be China) ejected Britain, the erst-while leader in industrial development, from the second, third and even fourth position in production.'[7] More recently the United States has become a reluctant member of the club. For example, in 1963, the rate of interest was raised to restrict an outward flow of funds even though the domestic interests of America would have been better served if the rate had fallen.

In looking at the problems of the gold exchange standard as a whole, it is of interest to reflect that the common element in all three of its characteristic dilemmas is a lack of net international liquidity in the key currency countries. If America and Britain are somehow able to reduce the deficit-inducing bias inherent in their problems—perhaps by cutting all long-term capital outflows—and instead run balance of payments surpluses, then the force of the dilemmas facing them would become progressively less pressing. If there is a lessening of monetary uncertainties from continued balance of payments surpluses in the key currency countries, the repatriation of dollar and sterling exchange brings the world back towards holding gold only. In this case the rest of the world would have fewer reserves and the outcome could be a reasonably stable international monetary climate, combined with a relatively stagnant international

---

[7] *Unequal Partners*, Vol. 2, *op. cit.*, p. 267.

economic environment. Alternatively, if the net reserve position of the United States and the United Kingdom should deteriorate, there is the danger of monetary collapse and financial chaos. In fact, if the world is to maintain the gold exchange standard as an operative system then, as it now stands, the mechanism must balance itself on a tightrope between these unacceptable alternatives.

That the world is actually trying to perform such a balancing act calls for some comment. The immediate reaction, of course, is to ask—why? The answer seems to be that the theories of those seeking to improve the system are so far apart that fundamental agreement is impossible. The range of disagreement between the views of the traditionalists—who want to move back to an earlier system—and the revolutionists—who want to leap forward to a new one—seems so wide that the only compromise is a hybrid form of the pre-1914 system. But the compromise itself becomes the rallying point of a third group which sees virtue in maintaining existing institutions and the *status quo*.

At one extreme, then, in the triangle of interests are the traditionalists. This group supports the idea of a return to the pure gold standard for they see much virtue in the self-regulatory mechanism of the nineteenth century model. For this group the basic element of order is discipline, and monetary discipline in the pure gold standard centres upon equilibrium in international payments. But the gold exchange standard, by its very nature, can expand only through disequilibrium. Equilibrium in the balance of payments in the key currency countries is not helpful to the gold exchange standard. The United Kingdom and the United States need to be in deficit if the key currency component of reserves is to grow. According to the "traditionalist" view, the United States and the United Kingdom therefore escape monetary discipline, and this in turn can bring monetary disorder to those countries holding dollars and sterling as reserves.[8] It follows, according to this view, that the only way of returning to sound finance is through reintroducing the pure gold standard of the last century, with gold at a higher price

---

[8] See, for example, Jacques Rueff, "The West is Risking a Credit Collapse", *Fortune*, July 1961.

to compensate for the loss of dollars and sterling as international exchange.

The aim of the revolutionary group is quite different, for they wish to create a new international paper obligation and thereby replace the use of gold as money (either gradually or immediately). Although the traditionalist group postulates the use of gold by itself so as to preserve economic purity, the revolutionists in contrast would prefer to get rid of gold entirely so the new era of economic purity can start! But disagreeing about the monetary functions of gold does not prevent the traditionalist and revolutionary groups from being united in considering the gold exchange standard as unsatisfactory. Perhaps this is one reason why the few attempts at making fundamental improvements to the gold exchange standard have had little success. Both extremes would prefer to be rid of the system entirely: both would appear loath to improve it in case it should become a more permanent feature of the institutional structure, perpetuating the characteristics considered undesirable. But the main cause of concern for the revolutionary group about the present-day system is with the immediate danger of monetary collapse. Triffin, for instance, sees the problem largely as one of delicate see-saw balance where doubts about the exchange rate stability of a reserve currency may cause a transfer of loyalties through currencies towards gold as the exchange component is progressively liquidated.[9]

Notwithstanding the undoubted faults of the gold exchange standard, those supporting the *status quo* are in the strongest position and this is simply because the two alternative groups in the triangle of interests carry little effective weight. On one side a return to the nineteenth century gold standard is largely discounted as being out of step with contemporary economic and political philosophy, while on the other, any advance to new concepts of international monetary co-operation—including world central banking—at some point or another conflicts with present-day ideas of national sovereignty. In the circumstances the best approach to eventual monetary salvation (however indefinite) would seem to be obvious. The gold exchange

[9] *Gold and the Dollar Crisis, op. cit.*, p. 67.

standard must be improved, not only to take care of the more immediate monetary dilemmas but also to ensure that those economic problems—thrown up by a world of change—can also be tackled without restraint.

The big question is whether the existing system can even continue to muddle indefinitely along its present track.[10] It can do so according to the International Monetary Fund, the United States Treasury and a number of other less august bodies supporting the key currency approach. To stop disintegration, all that is needed is more and more exchange, mixed differently perhaps, but nevertheless applied faithfully to cover each new crack appearing in the international structure. But will this serve if, as critics suggest, the present gold exchange system is basically unsound? For if it is true that earnest international experimentation is directed towards preserving the hopeless, then besides any direct economic calamity looming up, there is also the danger of casting a shadow on the merits of any monetary co-operation amongst nations.

Despite the fact that some protagonists of the key currency approach deny the existence of an immediate shortage of international liquidity, no serious observer is sure about the ability of the existing mechanism to supply the longer-term world requirements.[11] Others take a less sanguine view of the present. The Brookings Institution, for example, looks at the matter subjectively and cautiously suggests: 'The amount of additional reserves that would be required to remove the international monetary constraint felt by countries that should be pursuing more expansionist domestic policies is, in our judgement, at least equal to, and probably greater than, the losses of reserves which other countries could stand without being constrained to pursue undesirable policies. If that view is correct, a mere shift of the existing volume of reserves would not remove undesirable constraints in the world as a whole. It would only reduce, or remove, them in some countries at the cost of increasing or imposing

[10] See Fritz Machlup, *Plans for Reform of the International Monetary System*, Special Papers in International Economics, Princeton University, No. 3, August 1963, p. 13.
[11] See Robert V. Roosa, "Reforming the International Monetary System", *Foreign Affairs*, New York, October 1963, p. 112.

them in others.'[12] Lamfalussy goes further and shows that a redistribution of reserves can have an adverse influence if the total is in short supply. In writing of recent trends he said, 'The redistribution of reserves may sooner or later reach a point where the United States will *no longer* have enough reserves and Western Europe will *not yet* have enough of them.'[13]

But whether there is an existing shortage or not—and the aim of this book has been to demonstrate such a shortage—there is at least universal agreement about the need for more reserves to meet future requirements. With prejudice in favour of a static gold price concept on the one hand, and a distaste for new non-metallic international obligations on the other, the liquidity base can be enlarged only through an expansion of borrowing facilities, including an increase in the number of key currencies held as reserves. The present-day endeavour is to accomplish an increase in lending facilities and borrowing rights on a wide front, not, it might be added, so much because of economic welfare considerations but simply because there is pressure on the existing monetary machinery brought about by a deficit in the United States balance of payments.

Expanding the gold exchange system by increasing the number of key currencies is in effect a particular form of blowing up the international credit structure. Holding key currencies as reserves is essentially the same as maintaining an ordinary banking account, for those central banks holding dollars and sterling as reserves are in effect granting the United States and the United Kingdom a loan repayable on demand. All the general problems concerned with any type of expansion of the credit base (which will be covered in subsequent paragraphs) therefore also arise with the expanded key currency approach. But this latter concept needs close and separate scrutiny, for if the gold exchange standard has a long-term predisposition towards producing monetary instability, it is necessary to be cautious about expanding the self-same system in the hope of then getting rid of the instability.

[12] *The United States Balance of Payments in 1968, op. cit.,* p. 235.
[13] A. Lamfalussy, "International Trade and Trade Cycles, 1950-60", in *International Trade Theory in a Developing World, op. cit.,* p. 268 (author's italics).

The expanded key currency approach seems to rest largely on the shoulders of the United States Treasury, the idea being its answer to one side of the liquidity dilemma which would arise with a surplus in the United States balance of payments. When America moves into surplus, the suggested policy is for the United States to accept the currencies of certain other countries as payment for the accruing net credits. Instead of reducing world reserves the surplus would then act just like a deficit by increasing them. Even if this seemingly sensible concept were possible—in the sense that those in deficit to the United States would willingly run into debt to America while still holding what they may consider to be excessive liquidity in the form of dollars —the whole idea nevertheless bypasses quite a range of banking and monetary considerations. On the banking side it is important to remember that a key currency is only worth holding if the issuing country has an international money market capable of absorbing all likely inflowing placements—a good key currency being a national money that would still be held internationally even if it had no specific reserve functions. A key currency country must therefore have banking and ancillary services of sufficient international stature not only to attract funds, but also to employ them profitably and to remit them readily to all corners of the globe. Should such facilities be lacking, as they were even in the United States in the early twenties, then the tendency is for reserves to gravitate to any other centre giving a better banking service. When the exchange rates of those countries with the best international money markets are under suspicion, then their banking pull diminishes in proportion to the calculation of exchange risks thought to be involved. If doubts about the future exchange rates in the major key currency countries are widespread, therefore, the movement of money to the country offering the most advantageous terms for the employment of short-term funds may well be limited. In other words, the additional key currency approach can only function if it is not doing its job of promoting monetary stability properly.

Currently New York and London are the only fully developed centres of international finance, and the single satisfactory way of increasing the number of key currency countries is to build up new competitive markets in other countries.[14] Yet for all the possible gains in banking profits, other countries may not wish to join the key currency club and thus experience the economic difficulties which crop up when short-term liabilities become so extended as to give the dilemmas outlined above. Even if the United States should, when in surplus, accept other national currencies without limit in settlement for its net credits, the issuing countries may be unwilling to make them fully convertible. According to one observer: 'In general, a foreign currency acquired by U.S. authorities can be used to support the dollar only if it drops in exchange value against that currency, but it probably could not be sold without permission from the monetary authorities of that country to support the dollar against other currencies. These currencies do not at this time serve as international media of exchange in the same way as the U.S. dollar does. . . .'[15]

Not only does the expanded key currency approach suggest the need to hold obligations less freely convertible than dollars (and value them as if this were not true), but as the dollar grows scarce and becomes stronger (with a surplus in the United States balance of payments) these new reserve currencies become weaker because the issuing country runs a deficit. Other countries, including the United States, may then feel progressively disinclined to accumulate such obligations as their attractiveness (or order of precedence) falls. A suggested technique for making all key currencies rank equally is to apply a gold guarantee to each of them. On the other hand, and as shown on page 108, guaranteeing the gold value of national currencies creates a bias towards permanently fixing the existing rates of exchange. Increasing the number of key currency countries, therefore, spreads wider the number of countries where any alteration in the rate of exchange becomes much more difficult.

The Bernstein suggestion for the creation of a new international currency by forming a Reserve Unit made up from fixed

---

[14] If this is the policy of the United States Treasury it must seem peculiar in New York banking circles.

[15] Walther Lederer, *op. cit.*, p. 25.

proportions of eleven important national currencies would perhaps go further and make any unilateral alteration in par values virtually impossible.[16] Here then is a system to increase reserves which adds to the need for them through freezing the rates of exchange in a widening array of important countries. Over the years and as the existing rates become more and more unrealistic, some countries will drift towards constant surplus while others experience near constant deficit and all the economic dilemmas inherent in being a key currency country. Those countries in continuing deficit would sooner or later be forced into dishonouring their obligations, whether it was a gold guarantee for their money held abroad, or their commitment to hold a stated percentage share of any new international currency made up from fixed proportions of national currencies.

It may therefore be assumed that few countries, if any, would be willing to give a gold guarantee or join in forming a new international obligation based on rigid par values. As a result any schemes for enlarging the number of key currencies must seek out some other technique to ensure that all national currencies used for reserve purposes are equally desirable. Before 1914, one of the real advantages of the gold standard was the lack of capacity or need to move money between different centres. In those times London was the unquestioned and sole centre of the world's payments system. The only switching likely to occur was therefore between sterling and gold, but as sterling was mainly held for commercial functions and gold was used for reserve functions, the international usage of the two currencies tended to be complementary to each other rather than substitutes for each other.[17] With different forms of money performing different functions, precautionary and speculative switching did not occur. Nowadays national currencies are held as international reserves along with gold, so more than one currency can fulfil the same function. Through enabling key currencies to be held as reserves, the gold exchange standard itself has set aside the complementary nature of the main international forms of money

[16] *A Practical Program for International Monetary Reserves, op. cit.*, p. 5.
[17] Gold and sterling were substitutable in the *domestic* economy of the United Kingdom in the nineteenth century. In this context the present-day system is directly opposite to the gold standard existing up to 1914.

existing before 1914. As long as the gold exchange standard remains and different currencies are substitutes one for the other rather than complementary to each other, it can therefore be expected that different moneys will rank in precedence. Enlarging the number of key currencies only adds to the magnitude of the order of sequence (and so to greater confusion) as lesser known—even if temporarily strong—currencies join the better known national moneys, which may be temporarily weak.

Not only is there a currency order of precedence, but with the expanded key currency approach, the ranking of different national currencies is likely to change profoundly if not continuously. A. C. L. Day, when considering dollars and sterling wrote: 'If there is a danger that one of the two main international currencies will lose its value (or its usefulness in some other way, such as the freedom with which it can be employed) relative to the other, then many of the countries which had been using the first kind of international currency for making payments and for holding reserves will find it prudent to switch their loyalty to the other. This switch in loyalties, with the violent disturbances it creates, is a large part of the explanation of the crisis of 1931'.[18] Extending the number of key currencies adds cumulatively to these latent dangers. With but one key currency, there is but a single potential switch—between gold and the key currency. With two key currencies, dollars and sterling, there is a possibility of three movements—between sterling and gold; dollars and gold; sterling and dollars. If three national currencies are used as international reserves, the potential number of unstabilizing movements rises to six, and with five key currencies the number of potential switches increases to no less than fifteen.

Indeed it may reasonably be concluded that it will prove impossible to expand the number of key currency countries in a manner which will add significantly to world reserves. Although a wider holding of national currencies could help to smooth international payments and in fact perform some reserve functions, the holding of a range of new key currencies in large amounts, and specifically as reserves convertible on demand,

---

[18] See A. C. L. Day, United Kingdom: *Committee on the Working of the Monetary System, Memoranda of Evidence*, Vol. 3, p. 72.

would (even if it were possible) soon end in complete monetary chaos.

Nevertheless, the expanded key currency approach is by no means the only method of increasing the international credit base. On page 48, mention has been made of some of the new credit facilities which have been grafted onto the existing monetary machinery. Many of these changes, along with the associated co-operation amongst central bankers, have proved most effective in preventing speculative attacks on individual currencies. By means of this co-operation, details of which are largely held secret in the hope of thereby increasing their effectiveness, the great monetary calamity of the inter-war years—when speculative attacks fed upon themselves—has so far been avoided. Indeed the co-operation among central banks and the International Monetary Fund has to date proved so successful that speculators would appear nowadays to mount only a half-hearted attack in times of crisis, thus in fact minimizing the urgency of effective counter-action.

Yet it would be optimistic to suggest that increased borrowing facilities can solve the longer-term liquidity problems facing the free world or, for that matter, those present difficulties concerned with transferring capital to the poorer countries. Credit, of the type made available through the International Monetary Fund, Basle Agreements or other clubs of lenders and borrowers, is only used when a reversal of an outward flow of funds over a short period is expected. In the words of one Deutsche Bundesbank Report: 'The Central Bank's swap and similar credit facilities are by their nature in most cases short-term. For this reason they are normally used only in situations where there is reason to suppose that the outflow of funds will be reversed in a relatively brief period.'[19] An extension of credit cannot supply the longer-term needs of the international economy, for each addition to the lending arrangements now in vogue (including the expanded key currency approach) presupposes a shortening of the total uncommitted or net reserves available in the collective hands of surplus countries. These countries in turn may run into balance of payments deficit and start calling in outstanding

---

[19] *Report of the Deutsche Bundesbank for the Year 1962*, p. 27.

debits. There can then be a chain reaction of default, particularly among those countries which have borrowed short-term while maintaining long-term lending. In other words, unless long-term capital transfers are tailored to meet monetary considerations rather than economic needs, an over-extension of short-term credit facilities could ultimately lead to a financial crisis of the very type the protagonists of such schemes wish to avoid.

From the economic point of view the international monetary system needs "owned" reserves rather than "borrowed" reserves. The disequilibrium in world payments between the industrial countries and the primary producing countries and the need for a transfer of resources to the underdeveloped countries could last for several decades.[20] Equilibrating capital movements, particularly massive in total over such an extended period, cannot be transferred satisfactorily on the basis of an ever-increasing pyramid of credit. The United States, for example, is placing itself in a most precarious and unfavourable position if it should seek to continue borrowing short-term to maintain long-term lending. Such latent dangers, inherent in expanding the exchange component of reserves and a growing pyramid of credit, are not present with gold. The acquisition of newly mined gold, or an increase in the price of gold, gives a *net addition* to international reserves for it occurs without an increase in international debt. The late Per Jacobsson touched upon this point in stating: 'When international liabilities are settled in gold, this is a definite and final settlement, leaving no credit nexus as is the case when settlement is made in other ways. Gold payments are less complicated, and this is an advantage.'[21] For this reason too it may be just as well that sovereign nations feel disinclined to include borrowing facilities as part of their reserves, and this goes beyond the inconsistency with the literal meaning of the word "reserves". Because "owned" reserves do not need to be repaid, there is no need for a subsequent balance of payments surplus which by contrast is needed to ensure the effective repayment of "borrowed" reserves.

[20] See Chapters V and VI.
[21] Per Jacobsson, *The Market Economy in the World of Today,* American Philosophical Society Memoir, Vol. 55, 1961, p. 74.

I

REINFORCING THE MECHANISM

The fundamental needs of the international monetary system are achieved when the economic and monetary problems facing the world are both solved. Any increase in liquidity should on the one hand lubricate the mechanism for a growth in trade and capital transfers and, on the other, ease—or preferably solve—the monetary dilemmas of the key currency countries. Expanding the credit base, either by increasing the number of key currencies or by the other methods currently under discussion, cannot make a significant contribution to either of these requirements. The essential requisite is for a growth in the amount of "owned" reserves and this can only occur in two ways. Firstly, a new international paper obligation could be created and given away according to some pre-arranged formula. The formula would have to make particular allowance for the United States —it would need to recognize America's important role as a major exporter of capital and military aid, as well as taking into account the necessity for easing America's dilemmas in relation to the dollar and the gold exchange standard. In short, the United States would need to obtain by far the greater share of the initial handouts and this may prove politically difficult.

The second method is by increasing the price of gold and this has at least two immediate advantages over techniques of creating a new international paper obligation. For one thing there is no need to quarrel about any formula for sharing the windfall gains: rather ham-fistedly it goes to those countries (and individuals) lucky enough to already possess gold. Such a distribution of gains may not necessarily be the most laudable but it would seem to be the most adroit. This leads to the second point. Raising the price of gold removes any awkward situation which might otherwise arise in establishing the monetary precedence between the new international currency and gold. If a new international currency is not created, there is no possibility of adding to the monetary difficulties which can occur when a change in the order of monetary precedence prompts a similar change in the composition of reserves. A revaluation of gold in terms of all national currencies is both administratively easy and clear-cut. It leaves no room for confusion or argument.

There are other perhaps more positive reasons which give the advantage to an increase in the price of gold. As a compromise, it should find favour with the tangled triangle of opinions advancing varied schemes for a monetary Utopia. The key currency group can support it without lessening their own argument, for an improved gold cover strengthens the weak links in the present-day gold exchange standard. Supporters of the pure gold standard would agree that there can be no possible return to the traditional gold standard without a revaluation. Those favouring an international paper money standard may well countenance the measure as a policy of transition pending the development of a more sophisticated international monetary system and a stable world political climate. Reasonable political and economic stability is needed to ensure there is no downgrading of a new unproved international money if a crisis should provoke a switch of affections towards gold (thus in effect also making it impossible for a new international money to meet the task implied in the gold exchange standard of rationing gold). In point of fact, making gold more valuable in terms of price paradoxically reduces its standing as a reserve hoard, there being more to go round. In these circumstances gold and a new international currency, gradually introduced, are much more likely to rank equally in precedence.

But would a revaluation of gold solve the United States payments deficit *plus* the world liquidity problem at the stroke of a pen? The most recent figures show the United States gold reserves as being equivalent in value to 3 per cent of the United States gross national product, or to look at the matter in a different way, to about ten days' gross income. With gold revalued to, say $100 an ounce, the "income" of the United States is increased by 5 per cent *in the year* of the revaluation, so no great direct domestic change is likely either in the inflationary sense or in any other way.

It is the external position which is altered radically. At $100 an ounce United States reserves would increase to a total of approximately $45 billion. There would be no difficulty in paying off all the short-term dollar assets owned by foreigners, if this was desired. Paradoxically, and in contrast to the generally accepted view, the revaluation strengthens the dollar, for its cover in terms of gold is then much more assured. With such a price rise the United States has no need to worry about the monetary dilemmas imposed by the limitations of the gold exchange standard (as is the case when it operates on a small base of "owned" or net reserves).

As the richer creditor countries collectively have by far the greater proportion of all the gold held in official stocks, this technique therefore gives an increase to net reserves, where it can be utilized in facilitating a capital outflow without too much concern for the balance of payments position in the meantime.[22] Expressed differently it can be said that because of the need to increase living standards in the wake of the twentieth century technological revolution, traditional ideas about self-regulatory balance must be set aside for the next decade or two until the poorer countries themselves reach take-off and are in a position to fulfil their debt obligations.[23] If military aid is included in the calculation, then the need for an increase in total liquidity is reinforced—for this form of capital outflow is never normally matched by a subsequent inflow.

In regard to the extended period of capital transfers needed to maintain and expand the world economy on one hand, and the size of the "owned" reserves required to ensure international monetary stability on the other, the world increase in reserves should be quite large compared with the existing net total. Increasing the price of gold to $100 an ounce trebles the net reserves of the free world, approximately. Annual additions to the supply would probably increase slightly more if the price rise should lead to increased output from the mines. In these circumstances, and with net free world reserves at around $120 billion (which is itself about one-fifth of the United States gross national product in a *single* year) and annual increases at around $5 billion, the great liquidity limitation threatening economic growth

---

[22] In other words, in seeking to meet the objectives embodied in the Stamp Plan (where the increase in reserves goes to the debtor countries) the new reserves go instead to the creditor countries in the first instance.

[23] With an increase in the price of gold important direct benefits would accrue to the reserve position of some underdeveloped countries—and particularly India. Private gold hoards in India total approximately $3 billion (at $35 an ounce) and an increase in the dollar price of gold might stimulate a transfer of the metal from private to official hoards.

and monetary stability would be removed. As mankind in the present state of its philosophical development seems willing to accept and accumulate only gold in unlimited amounts (and even then to value it so highly as to hold onto it guardedly) no other form of obligation can be conveniently created to fill such vast needs without having its utility impaired.

CHAPTER VIII

INCREASED GOLD RESERVES
FOR FREE-WORLD OBJECTIVES

Some countries have achieved affluence through the great technological changes of the last century. The dynamic growth within a few countries has not, however, overflowed to help the great majority of nations. In the nineteenth century, in fact, the traditional craft industries of many poorer countries were frequently swamped out as an improving spread of transport took the new products of Bradford and Sheffield to the four corners of the globe. At that time the industrializing countries of Western Europe could pay for their imported raw materials with their own new mass-produced commodities. In the twentieth century, though, many of these raw materials—the export of which in the nineteenth century gave many poorer countries some balance of payments support—have become increasingly obsolete as the technological revolution has extended even further into the creation of synthetic alternatives. This inexorable process has been one factor tending to widen the disparity between the living standards of the rich and those of the poor countries; first, as the industrial revolution broke up the traditional craft industries of the less developed nations and later as the plastics revolution at least partially replaced many of their traditional exports.

Unless the balance is repaired, the gap in living standards between the relatively rich and the relatively poorer countries may well widen further as the poorer nations become increasingly bogged down with population problems and difficulties with increasingly obsolete exports. Instead of the demarcation between patrician standards of consumption and those of the proletariat occurring so markedly within the boundaries of individual nations, the contrasts in living standards will be more and more between the two main groups of nations—the developed and underdeveloped.

The present study has attempted to demonstrate that the acquisition of an improved international monetary system is a necessary precondition for mounting a serious attack on many of the welfare problems of the world economy. Even with the best of motives, the drive to industrialize the poorer countries—and the necessary adaptation in all countries to the resultant changes in the world economy—will be impeded if the appropriate monetary facilities are lacking. It is not that the international monetary system needs to change profoundly before being able to service the objectives of economic welfare. The single fundamental requirement is a vastly increased level of reserves over the next decade or two. If the richer countries take the initiative, it may be possible to achieve a satisfactory balancing of the trade and payment between the industrial countries on the one hand and the primary exporting countries on the other. At the present stage of world economic growth, the flow of capital from richer to poorer stands at the cornerstone of international welfare.

But a transfer of productive developmental capital has a habit of depressing the balance of payments of the capital exporting countries and it may take a decade or more before this disadvantage works itself out. Most deficits nevertheless are assumed to be quickly reversed so the monetary mechanism needed for such a purpose has not been forthcoming. Economic theory, for example—perhaps through a hangover from the gold standard generalities—normally includes the assumption that balance of payments deficits will be corrected in one or two years. Banking circles imply support to such a proposition and the International Monetary Fund, for instance, has a maximum of five years on its deficit correcting loans. Temporary imbalances in a country's foreign accounts are usually assumed in theory to be put right by equilibrating reserve or capital movements, and more lasting deficits by an exchange depreciation or some other appropriate policy like import controls—or even, deflation. But in the real world, alterations in the exchange rate or an increase in unemployment (arising from deflation) can be impeded by political or domestic welfare considerations. In such circumstances international capital movements promoting world

127

economic growth must play second fiddle to domestic objectives.

Domestic and international objectives can only hope to be in unison when there are sufficient reserves around to ensure that any factors limiting the flow of capital are minimized. But even then some transfers may not fit any repayment period. Capital payments in the form of reparations, or current payments for the stationing of military personnel or taking holidays abroad—or even for effective forms of economic aid—may curse the assumed neatness of the theoretical analysis. In these cases and in contrast to most commercial transfers, the balance of payments debits associated with the outward payments are not subsequently off-set by any form of credit.

FREEDOM FOR POLITICAL OBJECTIVES

Once again an unsatisfactory mechanism leads to a conflict of interests. Although a contraction of the United States balance of payments deficit, for example, may be necessary to allow America to check the fall in her gold reserves, a continuation of certain programmes like military aid—which tends to worsen the deficit—may be necessary for political reasons. Even though the pros and cons of defence commitments in foreign countries are scarcely part of a book on economics, the balance of payments consequences of military expenditure have a distinct bearing on the subject. Loans for economic development and private capital transfers have a different balance of payments influence from international defence spending. Sooner or later investments of the former type will be more than returned in interest or capital re-payments. All that is needed in such cases is sufficient reserves to cover the outflow of funds and their subsequent return. De-fence expenditure abroad, by contrast, produces no income and no return to the supplier, and can have a range of devastating economic influences (along with helpful ones for some recipient countries).[1]

[1] Foreign tourism is another ever-increasing form of external expenditure with a somewhat similar balance of payments influence. Certain countries, such as the United States, tend to be in constant deficit on tourist account while others may enjoy a constant surplus. In 1962 tourist receipts equalled 18 per cent of exports in Italy, 19 per cent in Switzerland and no less than 65 per cent of exports in Spain. (*The Economist*, London, 11 January 1964, p. 124.)

Firstly, from its very nature (and if other things remain equal) the country supporting the major part of international defence expenditure ends up having its balance of payments position depressed compared with other industrial countries. Over the period from 1954 to 1962, for example, the United States spent $15 billion for military purposes in Europe and over that time European reserves rose $13 billion so that, 'while military receipts from the United States have been only one of a number of factors, they have had an important effect in enabling these countries to run balance of payments surpluses and to accumulate reserves.'[2] Those countries which shoulder most commitments as a consequence of having the highest national income in either total or per head terms may end up being relatively weak in the exchanges. No matter what their relative wealth or income, the relative external economic strength of those countries with the highest international defence commitments is then affected adversely compared with those who may have benefited from the assistance. Those which carry the responsibility of leading the free world end up in a strange predicament. At the moment, and because gold is scarce and the holding of exchange gives holding nations power over the key currency countries, the economic strength of nations is equated more and more with the ability to gain reserves.

If countries with great economic strength—such as the United States, possessing a gross national product over 60 per cent in excess of all of Western Europe combined—should need to make their influence stronger internationally, reserves must be sufficient to meet the task. The importance of reserves for enabling countries with the greatest economic strength to exert a corresponding influence in world affairs is thrown into relief when a country so opulent as the United States has to live out of the garbage-can abroad. For instance the United States maintains all kinds of irksome restrictions upon the spending of its defence personnel serving abroad, with the aim of obtaining a balance of payments saving of $50 million a year.[3] But such penny-pinching is ironic, for the saving represents well under one-hundredth of one per cent of the American gross national product (and even

[2] The Brookings Institution, *op. cit.*, pp. 194, 195.
[3] *ibid.*, p. 199.

K

then it is not a saving in total expenditure—for that could well increase—but simply a saving in terms of foreign currencies).

Indeed the process goes further, for since the United States is also a key currency country, its international policy objectives tend to be self-defeating in the very execution. There is the general problem of seeking to ensure that foreign governments which hold dollars in large amounts do not convert these sums into gold, and the achievement of this aim can leave America prey to subtle or open political blackmail. In losing freedom of action while trying to maintain its influence abroad, America has to attempt to get the best of both worlds. But this may well prove impossible. The Brookings Institution estimates that between 1964 and 1968 American defence expenditure abroad will adversely affect the United States balance of payments by a total of no less than $8·1 billion—after taking appropriate steps to plug all possible leakages.[4] But this sum is more than one-half of the total United States gold stock at the end of 1965, and in turn means that the nature of the United States defence operations abroad could in the longer run be dictated by balance of payments considerations just as much as by military motives. If an important reason for not raising the level of reserves with an increase in the price of gold is to avoid helping Russia economically, then it must surely be strange indeed since the alternative policy scarcely seems likely to strengthen the United States militarily!

Although the danger is that of ending up with the worst of all worlds, the United States seems to be giving little consideration to resolving these problems through creating more reserves—either through a satisfactory new international currency devoid of a credit nexus, or through raising the price of gold. In fact a consideration of either of these alternatives is practically taboo in official circles, where a speedy correction of the deficit is the policy objective. Success in this direction in turn implies an outflow of capital and a level of commercial expenditure below the optimum needs of the international economy. It is worth while assessing further the motives for such behaviour, because this policy threatens the possible avenues along which the poorer

4 *ibid.*, p. 207.

countries can escape from poverty and endangers the level of world economic activity more generally.

Instead of being the hardest currency in the world, and as good as gold, the continuing American deficit relative to its gold hoard has made the dollar progressively weaker. In banking and treasury circles particularly, the deficit is seen as something intrinsically evil, for blame about the weakness of the dollar is placed much more with the United States deficit than with the attempt to operate the gold exchange standard with limited facilities.[5] So instead of building a better system, efforts are directed towards mending cracks in the existing structure. An associated reason for this lop-sided concentration seems to be that a deficit stretching out beyond the traditional two to four years, besides being considered "unsound finance", is in any case assumed by bankers to be simply impossible, implying as it does the obtaining of something for nothing. When talking about the "financial soundness" of a deficit in a key currency country like the United States, it is difficult to be objective. It all depends upon whether other countries are both willing and anxious to hold additional dollar I.O.U's instead of insisting upon gold as settlement for any net excess of claims. For reasons outlined in this book, no country is willing to accumulate national currency obligations as reserve assets indefinitely, and this, rather than considerations of "sound finance", is the immediate dilemma of the gold exchange standard and of the United States. A continuing deficit becomes impossible because the dollar itself needs more backing of internationally acceptable liquidity.

Plans for expanding the volume of international reserves can be reduced to a choice of three alternatives. There are schemes on the lines of the Keynes Clearing Arrangements for expanding the international credit structure through some form of international central banking.[6] Secondly, the price of the only purely international currency—gold—can be increased in terms of national currencies. Thirdly, there can be an increase in the variety of national money used as international money. With the

[5] A few short years ago the deficit was something intrinsically good.
[6] See, *Proposals for an International Clearing Union*, 1943, Cmd. 6437, H.M.S.O.

world central bank plan, an international agreement is necessary, for some amount of national autonomy must be handed over to an international body. With a revaluation of gold the world can obtain increased reserves without international co-operation in certain circumstances—as in the thirties, for example. The third alternative, which is an expansion of the key currency component of the gold exchange standard, can occur quite independently of any conscious planning. Thus an extension of the key currency approach has one fundamental advantage. Nevertheless, as shown in Chapter VII, it is certainly anything but satisfactory and is clearly potentially unstable. The irony of the situation is that the world may continue to use—or try to use—a discredited monetary concept just because there is a lack of agreement (even within the borders of each country) about which of the alternative solutions, if any, should be introduced.

Gold is free from the two limitations present with other forms of money and this is its great intrinsic advantage. It is automatically acceptable, for as shown by the history of the thirties in both America and Russia, it does not lose utility no matter how much of it has been accumulated.[7] In addition, being without a credit link, gold has no assumed or implied promise for repayment in any other money. Being free from the possibility or creation or manipulation by an issuing authority, the metal represents the final store of monetary value. If a new international paper obligation is to have these specific characteristics, two conditions therefore need to be fulfilled. Firstly it must take the place of gold as the final store of monetary value and this makes it necessary to demonetize the metal, for otherwise gold may continue to rank highest in monetary precedence no matter what the pleadings of international monetary authorities may be.[8] Then, secondly, the issuing authority must make the obligation available outright without a credit nexus. If this is not done, the growth in total liquidity will be in terms of gross reserves rather

[7] This property of gold, unique amongst all commodities, is certainly irrational in terms of economic theory and perhaps helps to explain why so many economists, instead of being eager to use this irrationality to best advantage, in fact themselves behave irrationally in trying to get rid of gold entirely.

[8] But see also footnote, page 109.

than net reserves, as the new money is paid out in exchange for existing obligations.

In this study the aim has not been one of disparaging those seeking to extend central banking procedures beyond national boundaries. Indeed the visionary schemes for establishing new paper international money could be the most sensible method of solving the problems covered in this book, if the two essential conditions outlined above could be fulfilled. But in any case, while the economists draw up blue prints for monetary Utopia, the politicians and bankers tread their cautious steps on traditional grounds. Where marking time is the norm, a leap forward to a totally new arena of monetary affairs represents a kind of slaughter: a killing off of all the instilled beliefs of the international banking order, so that if a few are willing to try, they are soon discarded and disgraced as heretics.

Sooner or later there will probably be a revaluation of gold, for since there is little likelihood of a satisfactory supra-national money being devised and accepted in the near future, there is simply no international medium of exchange other than gold with automatic, continuing and assured acceptability in all countries, whatever their living standards or political complexions. The great danger for economic welfare is not about the kind of reserves or the type of monetary machinery, for since all monetary schemes are the servants of mankind—or should be—there is no virtue in being particularly biased in favour of one of any alternatives if each does the job equally well. It is just that because of the continuing disagreements about the monetary therapy, nothing at all is likely to be planned and executed on a scale sufficient to meet the needs of the international economy. The increase in the price of gold could ultimately come by default, as in the thirties through a cycle of devaluations. Against this background it is important to note the views of the school unsympathetic to an increase in the price of gold but who at least, in the words of Triffin, see a revaluation of gold as 'far preferable indeed to the alternative solutions of world deflation or world restrictions'.[9]

[9] *Gold and the Dollar Crisis, op. cit.,* p. 79.

FREEDOM FOR ECONOMIC OBJECTIVES

If the desirable international aim is to let the United States maintain its economic aid and defence objectives, and to allow other industrialized countries to share the burden more equitably, then the sooner gold is revalued the better. This does not mean the United States or any other country can run a balance of payments deficit indefinitely. A revaluation of gold would merely allow a longer swing in the pendulum, more akin to that involved in financing non-commercial transfers (and even perhaps the more commercial forms as well), where the original balance of payments debit may take decades rather than years to be reflected in a corresponding credit. Indeed, as with military aid, there may never be a subsequent credit.

In any case, a large increase in the price of gold would not give the United States a huge increase in its uncommitted reserves after due allowance has been made for the gold needed to cover the domestic note issue and the dollar component of international reserves. In these circumstances, even with gold at $100 an ounce, the United States could run a deficit of $4 billion a year (itself about 0·7 per cent of the American gross national product) for the short period of only three and one-half years before its "free" gold would become exhausted. In other words, the world is not likely to have excessive levels of international liquidity even if the price of the metal should increase approximately three-fold. It should be remembered that if all interest-bearing exchange were repatriated in exchange for non-interest bearing gold, then with a three-fold increase in the price of gold, the total of reserves in the collective hands of the free world would only rise by just over 50 per cent.

Why then is the world, and more specifically, America holding back on the gold revaluation issue? There are many detailed points at issue which have been covered elsewhere.[10] But perhaps one of the most important elements explaining the mystery is that gold has been with mankind so long as to make it impossible to approach the topic without some display of emotion and misunderstanding. It is difficult for nations to look at the issue

[10] See Ian Shannon, *The Economic Functions of Gold*, Melbourne, F. W. Cheshire, 1962, Chapters VIII and IX.

objectively, for the very fact that gold has had strong links with mankind since pre-history and has indeed played a part in shaping history.[11] Like a demigod it stands at the pinnacle of metallic beauty and those lucky enough to possess it, whether now or thousands of years ago, have enjoyed great power over other mortals.

In the circumstances a national paper currency tied permanently to gold should absorb and display some of the glitter of the idolized metal. Dollars, for instance, become as "good as gold" so long as the exchange value between the two does not change in such a way as to favour the metal. With what must be the only example of price maintenance over three decades of war and peace, what was originally an expedient gold price in terms of dollars has now become a sacred price. But as dreams fade, reality intervenes. There is nothing sacrosanct about the present price of gold, either now or in 1934 when it was established during the early days of the Roosevelt Administration. But in view of all the philosophical and psychological overtones it is nevertheless difficult to remind ourselves that in some respects the dollar has nothing to do with gold. Although both mediums operate as money, gold is the sole international currency not used nationally and dollars, although used internationally, are first and foremost the national currency of the United States of America. Altering the price of international currency—which is not available to American citizens—in terms of United States currency has nothing specifically to do with the power and prestige of the dollar or the American nation.

Where then is the fundamental connection? National currencies are joined to each other through gold, a convenient measure of their exchange rates, and this link is expressed by a gold par value. The par value of United States currency is 0·888671 grams of gold per dollar and in such a sense foreign owners of dollars are holding gold I.O.U's of unguaranteed value. Increasing the price of gold means that each dollar buys less gold: with a tripling of the price, for example, instead of getting just on 0·9 grams of gold for each dollar, the quantity obtainable instead becomes less than 0·3 grams. With a gold revaluation,

[11] See J. M. Keynes, *A Treatise on Money*, London, Macmillan, 1930, Vol. II, p. 289 ff.

although those holding dollars as exchange reserves may refer to this changed par value as a "loss", the term is nevertheless misleading because each dollar continues to have the same command over goods and services. The only commodity in all the world becoming more expensive in terms of national currencies is gold—but this is unlikely to affect the greater proportion of mankind one way or the other in any immediate sense.

In fact the confused opinion that a "loss" results from revaluations would seem to arise from two further points. First, with a revaluation of the metal, those holding gold instead of dollars would enjoy a capital gain in terms of national currencies. On the other hand, gold, unlike most balances held internationally in the form of national currencies, does not earn interest and this is a disadvantage for gold holders. If since 1950 a central banker chose to hold dollars instead of gold, and kept reinvesting principal and interest each year at 3½ per cent per annum, then each $35 originally invested would now be equivalent to $61. So in a sense whether to hold gold or exchange is somewhat equivalent to the alternatives of holding growth or yield stocks.

The second point covers the confusion between *devaluation* and *revaluation*. As noted above, if there is a revaluation of all currencies against gold, there is no "loss". Dollars (and other national currencies) would continue to purchase about the same quantity of goods and services—and the command over resources is one of the fundamental reasons for holding reserves. But if the United States should devalue unilaterally, the story is quite different: then dollars will be worth less in terms of other national currencies and each dollar held as key currency will have less command over the resources of these countries. Because of the loss involved with a unilateral devaluation, it is important for the change in the price of gold to be universal for all important currencies.[12] Here indeed is one of the major obstacles, for seeking an agreement amongst nations about the future price of the metal could start a competitive scramble for the available stocks of gold amongst those nations anxious to obtain a capital gain.

---

[12] In any case there is no specific reason for a devaluation of the dollar. The United States has a strong trade surplus with other countries: the dollar is under strain simply because Americans have shouldered non-trade commitments.

Because of its position in the free world, the United States has to take the lead and the responsibility for the action. The present study has implied that doing nothing for fear of causing an immediate dissension is the irresponsible policy in the long run. More reserves are needed over the next decade or two to finance the lack of balance in the world economy: a big once and for all increase in the price of gold may well get the world over this hump.

Over the present century there have been many attempts at reducing the focal position of gold in the international monetary system. But since gold has remained in use as the residual store of value, the protagonists of alternative—and at times imaginative—plans feel the world does not heed their advice. These conclusions may well be true, but in the resulting confusion about the economic functions of gold, the monetary authorities have tended to become more cautious while underscoring the virtues of the metal. Owing to a lack of understanding, or perhaps to misunderstanding, the world ends up with the worst of all systems. Nations and individuals are unable to sink their differences sufficiently to evolve a totally new international monetary system. But then the countries of the world are unable to escape from the rigidities of an established tradition. By clear thought and decisive action on this issue, the free world could avoid the risks it is running and the losses it is suffering through the present process of muddling along.

INDEX

139

Index